REFLECTIONS ON CREATION, ORIGINAL SIN, AND "BIG EVIL"

REFLECTIONS ON CREATION, ORIGINAL SIN, AND "BIG EVIL"

A Theodicy

Charles L. Ladner

Copyright © 2020 by Charles L. Ladner.

ISBN:	Hardcover	978-1-7960-7620-2
	Softcover	978-1-7960-7619-6
	eBook	978-1-7960-7618-9

All rights reserved. No part of this book may be reproduced or transmitted in any form or by any means, electronic or mechanical, including photocopying, recording, or by any information storage and retrieval system, without permission in writing from the copyright owner.

The views expressed in this work are solely those of the author and do not necessarily reflect the views of the publisher, and the publisher hereby disclaims any responsibility for them.

Any people depicted in stock imagery provided by Getty Images are models, and such images are being used for illustrative purposes only.
Certain stock imagery © Getty Images.

Print information available on the last page.

Rev. date: 12/05/2019

To order additional copies of this book, contact:
Xlibris
1-888-795-4274
www.Xlibris.com
Orders@Xlibris.com
806108

CONTENTS

Introduction vii

I. Theodicy? 1

II. What is the Trinity? 6

III. Does God Exist? 10

    Does God Exist: The Big Bang. 11
    Does God Exist: The Anthropic Principle,
        The Fine-Tuned Universe. 14
    Does God Exist: Further Thoughts on the Proofs 18

IV. Original Sin, Evolution, and The Fine Tuned Universe 20

    Evolution, Original Sin, The Fine-Tuned Universe:
        Teilhard de Chardin 31

V. Comparison of this Theodicy with Selected Historical
        Treatments 36

    The Book of Job. 37
    Thomas Aquinas on Scriptural vs. Philosophical Authority 38
    Thomas Aquinas on Evil. 40
    Thomas Aquinas on the Proof of God's Existence by
        Intelligent Design. 41
    Thomas Aquinas on Man's Comprehension of God 42
    Thomas Aquinas on the Teleological Direction of the
        Universe 42
    Summary of Findings 55

VI. The Human Genome..57
    DNA and Abortion: Some Simple Lessons 60

VII. Final Thoughts 70
    The Question of Metaphysics...70
    Words and Concepts Appropriate to Their Times...................72
    Ideology as the Means by Which Satan Accomplishes
        His Objectives in the World. 73
    Is There a Teleological Direction to the Universe?..................80
    Conclusion: Things to Ponder. 83

VIII. Summary of the Argument...88

Bibliography...91

Introduction

"Ponder anew what the Almighty can do"

This small monograph is presented as a theodicy. A theodicy is an attempt to reconcile two seemingly irreconcilable realities: (1) The existence of evil and imperfection: (2) In a world created by a good and perfect God. If God is all powerful and all good, why then, did He create evil? Truly, a difficult subject. My thesis is that the traditional formulation of a theodicy is a false dichotomy. We cannot say that God is good. Neither can we say that all evil is bad.

As I was beginning to think through the matter, it became clear that it could not be addressed without traveling far afield from traditional theology. In the past, both theologians and philosophers have tackled the problem, only to arrive at hopeless failure, not uncommonly concluding that it was a "mystery" beyond human reason. So, with this in mind, and appreciative of the fact that a massive amount of new knowledge regarding the human condition has been unlocked by the cumulative efforts of scientists over the past century, I will be venturing on a consilient interdisciplinary approach traveling a long way from traditional thinking. While, it is a bold and presumptuous endeavor for someone like me, with limited credentials, to link together principles from different fields (science and theology) to form a comprehensive theory, it truly has been an intellectual journey opening new insights that were previously but vague and undefined. So, this is a different kind of theology. It takes much of its inspiration from science, yet as unorthodox as it may seem, it's findings had the effect of clarifying my faith. For what I came to realize was that while my conviction in the inerrancy of revelation is as firm as ever, many of the common interpretations that we hear every day, are encumbered by obsolete science and well-meaning, yet unverifiable and unsupported interpretations that are not only misleading, but in light of contemporary science, conducive to faith killing error. For some, they can present a barrier to belief.

As an example, the whole narrative of Adam and Eve, Paradise, the Apple, the Devil, the Fall, and most critically, Original Sin, has been proved to be nothing but a fairy tale with not a shred of historical truth. Who can believe this? For more than a century, geologists, anthropologists, cosmologists, zoologists, and more recently, molecular biologists have built a comprehensive body of knowledge demonstrating that life emerged on earth in the form of single cell organisms that through a three and a half billion year process leading to the emergence of a variety of humanoids that ultimately evolved into humans. There is neither biological nor geological evidence of paradise, or that all humans were derived from a unique couple.[1] Quite the contrary, evolutionary development was brought about by millions of organisms adapting to their environment over deep time. Nevertheless, while we now know that the story of Adam and Eve as understood by a literal reading of scripture may be historical error, the concept illuminated by the narrative that all humans are possessed of a fundamental defect in their

---

[1] In the words of Francis S. Collins, the head of the Human Genome Project and one of the world's leading scientists "…studies of human variation, together with the fossil record, all point to an origin of modern humans approximately a hundred thousand years ago, most likely in East Africa. Genetic analysis suggest that approximately ten thousand ancestors gave rise to the entire population of 6 billion humans on the planet…The real dilemma for the believer comes down to whether Genesis 2 is describing a special act of miraculous creation that applied to a historic couple that had walked the earth, or whether this is a poetic and powerful allegory of God's plan for the entrance of the spiritual nature (the soul) and the Moral Law into humanity." In: Francis S. Collins. *The Language of God, A Scientist Presents Evidence For Belief,* (New York: Simon & Schuster, Inc. 2006), 207.

tendency to frequently act in ways that we define as evil, is certainly correct. Atheist may call this "the selfish gene"; we call it Original Sin.

This is a sample of what you will find in the following pages. If revelation is true and science is true, then there should be no conflict between them. We might, therefore, be well served to interpret scripture with the aid of science. This, of course, implies that we must abandon many long cherished explanations in exchange for what may appear to be cold, hard scientific fact. If we do so, we will find that theological concepts like Original Sin may not be exactly as presented in the Bible or as interpreted by subsequent exegetes, but we will see they most assuredly remain indisputable truths.

The overarching theme of this essay is the question of theodicy. However, it is a theodicy rooted in two principals:

> <u>First</u>. God cannot be known by man. Central to this thesis is the Old Testament lesson that God is unknowable. My restatement is: *That between humans and their creator, there is an unbridgeable ontological chasm which makes the Creator God forever incomprehensible.* Not only is this statement consistent with traditional Church teachings, but also, it is an unavoidable consequence of the recent advancements of scientific learning of which we all have become increasingly familiar.
>
> <u>Second.</u> The notion that many of the traditional interpretations of scripture have been made irrelevant by the development of contemporary scientific knowledge is a fundamental principal driving this analysis. From this, it would seem to be self-evident that scriptural interpretations, where applicable, should be updated. And in consequence, such teachings, when illuminated by the insights of contemporary science, may once again become congruent with today's state of knowledge and thus become acceptable to the otherwise skeptical.

Along these lines, I have been pondering the unimaginable complexity and scale of the universe, knowledge of which, has only within the past thirty years, been assembled into what cosmologists term the Cosmological Standard Model. From this we learn of the origin of our universe and of its indescribable scale comprising an estimated 100 billion galaxies each one of which, on average, may have 100 billion stars. These are big numbers, so let me rephrase this statement. On average, there are 100 billion stars in a single galaxy. (The Milky Way is our galaxy, and our sun is one of the 100 billion stars in the Milky Way.) Yet, our Galaxy-the Milky Way-is infinitesimal when considered as only one of the 100 billion galaxies comprising the universe.

And then, coupled with these seeming impossibilities, I also have been pondering the incredible mysteries, and, the "unimaginable complexity" of the quantum world so long hidden from straight-forward investigation where a sub-atomic particle's physical movement and location is uncertain and is a function of probabilities; or where objects can be simultaneously a particle or a wave; or where movement of a particle can be replicated by another related particle at exactly the same time, without any known means of communication, no matter what the distance between them.

And in the biosphere, considering only humans, we have learned that each one of the 7.6 billion people on earth is made up of 37 trillion cells, as well as an equal or larger number of prokaryotes (bacteria) that enable our existence. [2]We have learned that evolution and the principals of natural selection are the fundamental rule of nature. And only as recently as 2003, with the completion of the Human Genome project, are we now gaining insight into the importance and function of human DNA and incomprehensible complexity of the embryonic stem cell.

These things, comprise a new body of knowledge that is truly revolutionary. Therefore, I am convinced that what is now happening right before our very eyes, is a universal paradigm shift of massive

---

[2] Eva Bianconi, Allison Piovesan et. al. "An Estimation of the Number of Cells in the Human Body", in *Annals of Human Biology, Volume 40, 2013-Issue 6*. (Accessed 8/5/2019. https://doi.org/10.31.3109/03014460.807878) 463-471.

proportions, greater even that the scientific revolution of the 16-17th centuries. It is one that will change our view of the world forever.

It is perfectly clear that our knowledge of the extraordinary complexity of the universe and everything in it has rapidly gone far beyond what was conceived only a few decades ago. It is also perfectly clear, to anyone who seriously thinks about it, that the implications for Christianity and religion in general, are profound. In fact, so profound, as to seem either a threat to our established theologies or, more hopefully, a vehicle to enhance, intensify, and deepen our appreciation of the majesty and creative integrity of our remote God. What these scientific advances can bring us is the conviction that God who creates such things from nothing, is truly unknowable, which holds out the potential to drive us to such an extreme degree of humility, that in consequence, we may hope for the opportunity to approach an intimacy with our mysterious God as we never before thought possible.

Nevertheless, my Church-the Catholic Church- continues to ignore such things, and insists that it fully knows everything there is to know, about the nature of God and His creative process. Even in the face of the unknowable, there is certainly no humility in this position. On the contrary, there is an element of pride, inasmuch as the Church asserts absolute certainty in the expression of such teachings. It sets forth these teachings in simple dogmatic statements that, because of the advancements in the physical and biological sciences, have long ago lost their meaning.

Yet, notwithstanding its erosion of credibility, the Church appears satisfied with the current state of affairs. Why? Well, among other things, because simple dogmatic statements are a good communication device, and while they fail to cleanly separate the message from the means of its delivery and are rooted in obsolete learning, they have worked for a long time to communicate to a mass populace. Even today, among population groups whose stage of intellectual progress is roughly comparable to that of 4th century Asia Minor, the church continues to make progress. But, among most of Europe, Asia, and the America's, it is a failing institution, losing adherents each year, especially among the youth. Moreover, if we fast forward a few decades as the rest of the world catches up, such also will be the fate of the Church in these areas as well.

Nearly a century ago, Pierre Theilhard de Chardin, Jesuit priest and paleontologist, began writing about this potential obstacle to faith. Among other things, he observed that we live in an unfinished universe, a concept that is alien to traditional theological formulations of a static universe, yet one that is fundamental to modern science. A good description of Theilhard's emerging theological insight is provided by Illia Delio, OSF:

> As a trained scientist, he (Theilhard) realized that we live in a culture deeply conditioned by the insights and theories of modern science but in the context of the church, its theology and liturgy, we live in a pre-modern world. Christian theology no longer has an effective cosmology that enables believers to relate to the world in its physical character in a way that is consistent with their religious symbols. In the stable medieval cosmos, Christian hope had a fixed aim, life with God in heaven above. But we have yet to reframe our hopes in light of an expanding universe where openness to the future and increasing complexity have supplanted the crystalline heavens. To evolve into a more fruitful and unitive life up ahead, we need to reshape our religious understanding of the world by engaging our faith with the best insights of science concerning the nature of the physical world.[3]

Currently, there are Christian scholars rethinking the old ideas with the goal of conforming the Scriptural interpretations with contemporary learning. Perhaps not surprisingly, it is not an impossible project to preserve and enhance the teachings of the Church within the context

---

[3] Illia Delio, OSF, "Introduction," in *From Theilhard to Omega, Co-creating an Unfinished Universe*, ed. Illia Delio OSF (Maryknoll, New York: Orbis Books, 2014), 2.

of modern science. After all, both are dealing with truth; and while not the primary undertaking of this study, the reader will see this theme woven throughout the following pages. [4]

> A note of caution: All that follows is based on contemporary theories in the physical, astronomical, and biological sciences. But, in the words of Thomas Kuhn, "The scientific theories that bulk so large in our daily lives are unlikely to prove final." Older theories, such as the Aristotelian-Ptolemaic geocentric concept of the universe, replaced by the Copernican theory in the 16th century, were believed with the same "resolute credence" that we now give our current theories. "Furthermore," he says, "they were believed for the same reasons: They provided plausible answers to the questions that seemed important." Scientific theories are "mutable", and what we believe to be true today may be nothing more than the building blocks upon which future truths are constructed. So, I think we should be sensitive to the fact that while science may be an aid in understanding theology, ultimately, it is faith that we must rely on.

---

[4] For an opinion, contrary to much of what is written here, especially on the subject of evolution, please see: *Humani generis*, a papal encyclical issued by Pius XII on August 12, 1950.

I

Theodicy?

Theodicy is defined by the Catholic theologian, John Haught as, "…the theoretical attempt to 'justify' the existence of God, given the facts of evil and suffering. If God is all good and all-powerful, then God must be able and willing to prevent life's suffering. But suffering exists. Why? Theodicy is the branch of theology that tries to answer this question."[5]

Another description of the problem, attributed to Epicurus (341-270BC) by Lactantius (250-325AD), is neatly summarized by David Hume as follows:

> Epicurus's old questions are yet unanswered. Is he willing to prevent evil, but not able? Then he is impotent. Is he able, but not willing? Then he is malevolent. Is he both able and willing? Whence then is evil?[6]

Typically, a theodicy will involve assumptions about the nature of God. In this paper, I will make no such assumptions. A theodicy also may include assumptions about the nature of evil, commonly dividing it into two categories: natural evil and moral evil. I will do the same,

---

[5] John F. Haught. *Is Nature Enough? Meaning and Truth in the Age of Science.* (Cambridge: Cambridge University Press, 2006). 172.

[6] David Hume. *Dialogues Concerning Natural Religion*, (davidhume.org: accessed April, 2018) 10.25.

but in a way, that departs from the norm. My approach will be through the lens of evolutionary theory, because I see this perspective not only as consistent with the Christian tradition, but also as surpassing other theodicies in both simplicity and clarity. This way of thinking, though highly empirical, does not necessarily deny other ways of knowing.

Certainly, in matters relating to religion, the creative imagination can yield truths inaccessible in any other way; but most especially, it is the mystical/spiritual experience that has produced the greatest depth of history's religious insights. I hope to draw on some of these insights in what follows.

The paper is divided into eight parts: (1) Comments regarding the idea of Theodicy, and a description of method. (2) A discussion of the Trinity as the essential nature of the Christian God. (3) A response to the question how we may know that God exists. (4) A theodicy, entailing a dissection of evil from an evolutionary perspective, including an analysis of the concept of original sin from the same perspective, and the teleological implications of both.

(5) A comparison of this theodicy to other, more conventional, treatments of the subject. (6) A discussion of the science of the Human Genome, and its implications for theology (7) Final thoughts on some of the more contestable matters. (8) A summary list of the argument. The order of presentation is important. In discussing the Trinity as the first topic, I will show substantial authority within the Catholic church for flexibility in the manner in which doctrine is presented. I will then surface doubts about our ability to comprehend the nature of God, and therefore doubts about the traditional Trinitarian formulations. Critical to this analysis, is an acknowledgment that, contrary to common opinion, we really do not know anything at all about the nature of God. Once having done that, an exercise that might be seen as even casting doubt on the existence of God, I will present evidence backed proofs that are so strong as to make it irrational not to acquiesce in the existence of God. Having thus prepared the way, I will then set forth a somewhat Darwinian, or more precisely, Teilhardian, theodicy that fits the preceding discussion. In this, the principal part of this paper, I hope to demonstrate that, in the words of Daryl Domning, a paleontologist and evolutionary biologist: *"Moral evil has literally evolved out of physical*

evil and it could not have been otherwise. (and) *Only by grasping this truth can the philosophical "Problem of Evil" and the riddle of theodicy be solved"*[7] This lengthy section will be followed by a discussion of the human genome, concluding comments on alternative notions regarding the problem of evil, and then a summary of the principal points.

To begin, I believe it essential to disclose that as a Roman Catholic, there are parts of the faith I have always found extremely difficult, not because they involve the mystery of the Divine, but because they fail to acknowledge it!

Among other things, these are the formulations of doctrines critical to faith that were drawn from, but never made explicit in revelation. Moreover, these widely held interpretations appear to be grounded in a curious resistance to acknowledge the impossibility of the human mind to comprehend the Divine presence. Therefore, in light of this skepticism, I should make it clear at the outset, that the underlying foundation of everything that follows in this paper can be summed up in my conviction, that there is an unbridgeable ontological incongruity between the created with the Creator, from which I assert that the Creator is incomprehensible.[8]

Church Fathers would not disagree with this formulation. They certainly express it better. Here is St. John of Damascus, writing in the 8th century:

> The Divinity, then, is limitless and incomprehensible, and this His limitlessness and incomprehensibility, is all that can be understood about Him…For He does not belong to the number of beings, not because He does

---

[7] Daryl P. Domning. "Theilhard and Natural Selection: A Missed Opportunity?" in Kathleen Duffy S.S.J., *Rediscovering Theilhard's Fire*, ed. Kathryn Duffy S.S.J. (Philadelphia: Saint Joseph's University Press, 2010) 192.

[8] I am not alone in this opinion, see Gregory of Nazianzus, as follows: "The Divine, then is boundless and difficult to contemplate; the only thing completely comprehensible about it is its boundlessness…The boundlessness can be considered in two ways: with regard to beginning and with regard to end; for what is beyond these, and not contained within them, is boundless" in, Brian Daley, S.J. Ed., *Gregory of Nazianzus,* (New York: Routledge, 2006), 120.

not exist, but because He transcends all beings and being itself.[9]

Many of the interpretations of revelation which I find inadequate are those that were set forth in fixed dogma by Church councils of the 4th and 5th centuries. Much later, some were further elaborated by various philosophers and theologians, but most especially, by Thomas Aquinas in the 13th century and by his Scholastic acolytes in later centuries. As for the Councils, it is a matter of historical record that some doctrinal formulations were enabled by secular political pressure. Others were influenced by the limited state of knowledge of the physical world that prevailed at the time. Some emerged out of anger and argument often motivated by clerical ambition. Some were even influenced by the prevailing secular philosophy of Neo-Platonism. And only a few were the product of prayerful humility. But, above all, the most disturbing aspect of these descriptions of God and God's message is the assertion by ecclesiastical authorities, consistently maintained over the centuries, that these formulations represent the absolute and unerring truth *in its totality*, and thus no other interpretation can be true. In the words and actions of the councilor fathers, other interpretations or advocates of such interpretations were anathematized, or said differently, they were declared to be evil and subject to Divine retribution. Pretty strong language, I think, for matters of conjecture.

So, what are these things? In my view, the standard presentations of the doctrine of the Trinity and the doctrine of Original Sin are grossly misleading by reason of their oversimplification. To a lesser extent, the same might be said regarding the treatment of Creation. It is my further opinion that while these doctrines represent interpretations appropriate to the state of learning at the time, it is the closed manner of their expression, along with the correlative insistence upon a precision inconsistent with man's ontological incompatibility with the divine, that constitute a fundamental problem. Again, John of Damascus can be helpful when he says:

> Furthermore, many of those things about God which are not clearly perceived cannot be fittingly described,

---

[9] John of Damascus. *Saint John of Damascus: The Fount of Knowledge, 1,4*. Translated by Frederick H. Chase, Jr. (Ex Fontibus.com: 2015), 172.

so that we are obliged to express in human terms things which transcend human order…But what the substance of God is, we neither understand nor can say. And so, it is impossible either to say or fully to understand anything about God beyond what has been divinely proclaimed to us, whether told or revealed, by the sacred declarations of the Old and New Testaments.[10]

Notwithstanding my criticism, there can be no denying the efficacy of oversimplification as a technique to communicate complex ideas. For two millennia, it has certainly worked well to spread Christianity throughout the world. Yet, the difficulty arising from conflating effective communication methodology with the search for truth, (which is really a conflict between the pastoral need for simplicity and the theological need for nuance), has clearly been won by those who resist any attempt to move beyond the patristic security blanket.[11]

In the following sections of this paper I will attempt to reflect on these matters in a way that substantially differs from the 4th century manner of thought because it will be from a perspective that incorporates the advancement in knowledge that has occurred since then. In doing so, I would like to think that if Origen, Ambrose, Augustine and Aquinas had been aware of such information, their interpretations might have followed similar lines; or at a minimum, they would have produced works considerably different from what they actually did at the time.[12]

---

[10] Ibid. 168.

[11] Despite the skepticism I express regarding the simple and anthropomorphic imagery used to describe the "incomprehensible" Godhead, I still pray daily to "The Father, Son and Holy Spirit," to "Our Father who art in heaven," and to "Holy Mary, Mother of God." Why? Habit, I suppose, but also because, it's the best we can do to describe what is truly unknowable.

[12] The Roman Catholic church asserts that, in addition to scripture, there are two additional means by which the Holy Spirit makes known religious truths: Tradition, and the Councils. Like Aquinas, I am skeptical of these sources, because they can be subject to error, misinterpretation, manipulation, imprecision, and outside influence. Aquinas believes they are secondary and too problematic to be trusted. See pages 38-39.

II

What is the Trinity?

Here my critique has to do with the reluctance of the 4th-5th century church to acknowledge the ontological incompatibility of God and Man from which logically flows the impossibility of understandings the nature of God. This subject is addressed in the following way, and in no uncertain terms, by Pope Benedict XVI, who, as we all know, is among the most careful and conservative of theologians:

> If the painful history of the human and Christian striving for God proves *anything*, it surely proves this: that any attempt to reduce God to the scope of our own comprehension leads to the absurd. We can only speak rightly about him if we renounce the attempt to comprehend him and let him be the uncomprehended. Any doctrine of the Trinity, therefore, cannot aim at being a perfect comprehension of God. It is a frontier notice, a discouraging gesture pointing over to unchartable territory. It is not a definition that confines a thing to the pigeon holes of human knowledge, nor is it a concept that would put the thing within the grasp of the human mind.[13]

---

[13] Joseph C. Ratzinger. *Introduction to Christianity*, translated by J.R. Foster. (San Francisco: Ignatius Press, 2004), 171.

This is a powerful statement and represents an invitation to carefully reconsider, or at least rethink, ancient formulations of doctrine in new and different ways. In my view, God, who from nothing, created the entire universe: its sub-atomic particles of matter, its fundamental forces, its laws of nature, space, light and even time itself, is of an order of being <u>inaccessible</u> to the human mind. He who describes himself simply as - *I am* - by his own definition tells us that he cannot be intelligible to humans. It simply is not possible.

Therefore, any presumption to go beyond Revelation, and to hypothesize anything at all about the nature of God, other than his existence, runs the risk of falling into the Anti-Galilean trap of making assertions unsupported by evidence. Moreover, the use of terms such as "hypostasis"(as was done by the 4th century fathers to describe each person of the Trinity in the original development of the Trinitarian concept) is straight out of Plotinus, as is the notion of a three part God. Plotinus, as we know, was the foremost pagan intellectual, and most widely studied philosopher of the patristic period. And it would not be surprising to find that his concepts and terminology, which were the most advanced "science" of its day, had seeped their way into the Council's formulations of the Trinitarian doctrine. In fact, the Catechism of the Catholic Church acknowledges its reliance on the pagan philosophical vocabulary in the following statement by Pope Paul VI:

> In order to articulate the dogma of the Trinity, the Church had to develop its own terminology with the help of certain notions of philosophical origin: "substance," "person" or "hypostasis," "relation," and so on. In doing this, she did not submit the faith to human wisdom, but gave a new and unprecedented meaning to these teams, which from then on would be used to signify an ineffable mystery beyond all that we can humanly understand.[14]

---

[14] Pope Paul VI. *Catechism of the Catholic Church.* (United States Catholic Conference: 1994), 251.

<u>So, given this clarification, one must ask: Why, if it was permissible to use Neo-Platonic concepts and terminology in the 4th and 5th centuries, and Aristotelian concepts and terminology in the 13th century, is it not equally permissible to use (for example) Darwinian concepts and terminology in the 21st century?</u>

Notwithstanding this question, we know there are different paths to enlightenment. So, to illustrate the possibility of another way to present the Trinity, here is a selection from Dante's *Paradiso*. You will notice no anthropomorphic allusions. No aroma of Neo-Platonism, and no attempt to reduce the Trinity to a "rational" formula. This is Dante in the presence of the Beatific Vision.

> Whoever sees that light is soon made such that it would be impossible for him to set that light aid for other sight because the good, the object of the will is fully gathered in that light…In the deep and bright essence of that exalted light, three circles appeared to me; they had three different colors, but all of them were of the same dimension, one circle seemed reflected by the second, as rainbow is by rainbow, and the third seemed fire breathed equally by these two circles.[15]

How much more powerful is the divinity represented in this near mystical vision than, for example, in the ridiculous anthropomorphic portrayal of God as an old man in Michelangelo's Sistine Chapel? Which might better capture the truth?

What is important about this, is that in trying to describe and understand the essential triune nature of God, the human mind runs up against an impenetrable wall — the wall of ontological separation. Therefore, if the most essential aspect of the Divine nature cannot be comprehended, how much less can we truly understand all his other so-called attributes. How irrational is it for us to assign to God such

---

[15] Dante Alighieri. *The Divine Comedy: Paradiso, Canto XIII*, translated by Allen Mandelbaum.(New York: Alfred A. Knopf, 1984) 540.

human characteristics as empathy, love, justice, compassion, jealousy, anger and vengeance?

My personal preference in describing the Trinity was articulated by the theologian Siegfried Wiedenhofer in a 2006 papal conference: "The Christian creed as a rule of faith is an affirmation…of God the Father, the Son and the Holy Spirit, or as one might say, of <u>"God over us"</u>, <u>"God with us"</u>, and of <u>"God in us"</u>.[16]

Finally, we should recall that while scripture says we are made in the image and likeness of God, we really do not know what that means. Moreover, what the bible <u>does not say</u> is that God is made in the image and likeness of humans. Thus, there is no scriptural authority for our assigning human or human-like attributes to God. We can no more say that he is loving and compassionate than we can say that he is jealous, angry and vengeful. We cannot say anything at all, because he is of a higher order of being to which, in our earthly lives, we cannot be reconciled. So, in the pursuit of a theodicy, when we try to attribute our notions of evil and justice to God's actions, we are in the land of absurdity.

---

[16] Siegfried Wiedenhifer. "Belief in Creation and the Theory of Evolution: Distinction and Point of Intersection", in Stephan Otto Horn, S.D.S. and Siegfried Wiedenhofer, *Creation and Evolution, A conference with Pope Benedict XVI in Castel Gandolfo*. Translated by Michael J. Miller, (San Francisco: Ignatius Press, 2008), 160.

III

Does God Exist?

While I emphatically deny the capacity of the human mind to comprehend the nature of God, I am equally confident that the human mind can be certain of his existence. We cannot know <u>what</u> he is, but we easily know <u>that</u> he is, and as we will see, it is indisputably the most logical and rational proposition that one can hold. What's more, as we will see, science proves it!

Well, the part about science may be a bit of an overstatement. But not much, for the scientific advances of recent years make it no longer a great leap of faith to believe in God. It is now only a small step. In fact, <u>it is now harder to believe that God does *not* exist, than it is to believe that He does</u>.

The scientific evidence for the existence of God is made explicit in two ways. The first is the Big Bang theory of the creation of the universe. The second is the argument from design based not on the apparently intelligent design of way natural things are made up, but rather on the initial conditions of the Big Bang and the correlative *process embedded* in both physical and biological nature, which is the cause, not only of the apparently intelligent design of natural things, but also their evolution over time, with each step appearing to be the product of intelligent design, and with each step revealing an emergent complexity. This is frequently called the Fine-Tuned Universe or the Anthropic Principle.

Does God Exist: The Big Bang.

Here we should start with some basic facts. The age of the universe is estimated to be 13.7 billion years. As for its size, it is currently estimated that there about 100 billion galaxies in the universe and within each galaxy there are approximately 100 billion stars.[17] If the average star is about the same size as our sun, which most astronomers believe to be the case, then we can say that each of those 100 billion stars within each of the 100 billion galaxies is so large that about 1,300,000 planet Earths could fit inside of a single star. The universe is really big. I don't know how to deal with numbers so immense, yet the Big Bang theory states that everything that comprises the universe was originally contained in an extremely small, less than atom sized object.

The Big Bang theory is a derivative of Einstein's 1916 publication of the General Theory of Relativity. It was first proposed in the late 1920's by George LeMaitre, later supported by the observational work of Edwin Hubble, and further refined by numerous theoretical changes and a constant stream of experimental and physical evidence including three NASA probes into deep space. By the mid 1980's the theory was considered to be the foundational basis for the current standard astronomical model of the universe.

The following is a description of the Big Bang singularity written by Robert Hazen, a leading researcher and prolific author, resident at the Carnegie Institute Geophysical Laboratory in Washington D.C

> The stage was set for our planet's birth…the Big Bang - about 13.7 billion years ago,… That moment of creation remains the most elusive, incomprehensible, defining event in the history of the universe. It was a singularity - a transformation from nothing to something that remains beyond the purview of modern science or the logic of mathematics.….In the beginning, all space and energy and matter came into existence from an unknowable

---

[17] David Christian. *Origin Story*, (New York: Little, Brown and Company, 2018), 10.

void. Nothing. Then something...Our universe did not suddenly appear where there was only vacuum before, for before the Big Bang there was no volume and no time. Our concept of nothing implies emptiness - before the Big Bang there was nothing to be empty in.

Then in an instant, there was not just something, but everything that would ever be, all at once. Our universe assumed a volume smaller than an atom's nucleus. That ultra- compressed cosmos began as pure homogenous energy, with no particles to spoil the perfect uniformity. Swiftly the universe expanded, though not into space or anything else outside of it (there was no *outside* to our universe). Volume itself, still in the form of hot energy, emerged and grew. As existence expanded, it cooled. The first subatomic particles appeared a fraction of a second after the Big Bang - electrons and quarks, the unseen essence of all the solids, liquids and gases of our world, materialized from pure energy. Soon thereafter, still within the first fraction of the first cosmic second, quarks combined in pairs and triplets to form larger particles including the protons and neutrons that populate every atomic nucleus. Things were still ridiculously hot and remained so for about a half a million years, until the ongoing expansion eventually cooled the cosmos to a few thousand degrees - sufficiently cold for electrons to latch on to nuclei and form the first atoms.

...Once upon a time, five billion years ago (about nine billion years after the Big Bang), our future real estate in the galactic suburbs lay halfway out from the Milky Way's center, at the uninhabited edge of a star-studded spiral arm. Little was to be found in that unassuming neighborhood, apart from a great nebula of gas and icy dust stretching light-years across the dark void. Nine parts in ten of that cloud were hydrogen atoms; nine parts in ten of what remained were helium atoms. Ice and dust, rich in small organic molecules and microscopic mineral grains, accounted for the remaining 1 percent.

…Ever so slowly, over the course of a million years, the swirling mass of premolar gas and dust was drawn inward. …As it collapsed and spun faster and became denser…Larger and larger grew that greedy hydrogen rich central ball, which ultimately swallowed up 99.9 percent of the cloud's mass. As it grew, internal pressures and temperatures rose to the fusion point, igniting the Sun.[18]

Well, here you have it, the description of the most advanced theory of the beginning of everything. It is, however, a synthesis that requires two acts of pure faith. In the first act of faith, science would have us believe that all the matter of the universe, the entirety of the 100 billion galaxies, is in the beginning, compressed within an object smaller than an atom. But that's not all, for the most current scientific findings now hold that the visible matter of the universe (the 100 billion galaxies) constitutes only 6.0% of the total matter and energy that makes up the universe, so it is the totality of this incomprehensible volume, (that which we can see, and that which we cannot see), that was subsumed in the primeval atom.

The second act of faith is that this beginning, this singularity, this primeval atom, had no cause. It is just there. Science has no explanation, nor any way of finding an explanation for its existence. It cannot find an explanation for its existence, because to do so would require the observer to be placed out of time and space, and we know that this is impossible because nothing preceded the Big Bang-no space, no time, nothing! Therefore, no alternative theory is possible because whatever hypothesis might be offered to inform such a theory cannot be tested by established means.. So, when people proffer the ideas of multi universes, or parallel universes, or an oscillating universe coming into and out of existence, they are off on flights

---

[18] Robert M. Hazen. *The Story of Earth: The First 4.5 Billion Years, From Stardust to Living Planet.* (New York: Viking Penguin, 2012). 6-14.

of imaginative fancy, whose proof lies beyond the experimental limits of the scientific empiricism upon which all science is based.

What then, requires greater faith, the scientific propositions I have just put forth (*i.e.* (1) the almost infinite volume of matter and energy compressed within the original primeval atom, combined with, (2) the impossibility of determining the cause of the original atom)? Or the simple fact of a creator God? Both demand an act of faith, so which one best meets the standards of Occam's Razor? It seems perfectly obvious to me that the simplest, more rational solution, is to accept the priority of a God of creation, if for no other reason that it entails the smallest leap of faith.

Does God Exist: The Anthropic Principle, The Fine-Tuned Universe.

For at least two millennia, the argument from design held sway as the most widely accepted proof of the existence of God. Typically, people observed the complexity of living things (especially humans), and from that data concluded that such well-designed beings could not possibly have arisen as a matter of pure chance. As one 19th century sage commented "if we find a watch, it is reasonable to conclude that there is a watchmaker."

However, with the discovery and development of the theory of evolution, it became apparent that the "watch" actually did come about by chance. The trillions of births, deaths, mutations, and adaptations, by all living things over billions of years that constitutes the process of evolution, producing near imperceptible changes in each species, leads gradually to the emergence of the complex entities that formed the basis of the old argument from design. Evolution, thus demolished the argument from design-at least- as originally formulated.[19]

Not long after the old argument from design disappeared, an entirely new variant of this argument, based on the physics of the Big

---

[19] Thomas Aquinas, in the 13th century, developed a more nuanced theory that looked to the forces that produced the design rather than the design itself, and, in a sense, anticipated the post-Darwinian argument from design-the Anthropic Principle. This will be discussed later in this paper.

Bang theory and late 20th century cosmology, began to make its way forward. This is the Anthropic Principle.

Briefly, the Anthropic Principle holds that human life could never have come about on this planet unless a long string of highly improbable physical coincidences occurred in the initial formation of the universe as an integral part the Big Bang singularity. The emphasis is on the highly improbable nature of each individual event which leads to an unimaginable improbability of all these events occurring together without some unknown external influence.

Physicist Sir Martin Rees, Royal Society Research Professor at Cambridge University, identifies six constant values that define everything from the way atoms are held together to the amount of matter in the universe. Inexplicably, these values are so precisely calibrated, that absent such fine tuning of any one of them, there would be no possibility of life, or for that matter, of the universe itself. Here is Martin Rees:

- o The cosmos is so vast because there is one crucially important huge number η in nature, equal to 1,000,000,000,000,000,000,000,000,000,000,000,000. This number measures the strength of the electrical forces that hold atoms together, divided by the force of gravity between them. If η has a few less zeros, only a short-lived miniature universe could exist: no creatures could grow larger than insects, and there would be no time for biological evolution.
- o Another number ε, whose value is 0.007, defines how firmly atomic nuclei bind together and how all the atoms on earth were made. Its value controls the power from the Sun and, more sensitively, how stars transmute hydrogen into all the atoms of the periodic table. Carbon and oxygen are common, whereas gold and uranium are rare, because of what happens in the stars. If ε were 0.006 or 0.008, we could not exist.
- o The cosmic number Ω (omega) measures the amount of material in our universe – galaxies, diffuse gas, and 'dark matter'. Ω tells us the relative importance of gravity and expansion energy in the universe. If this ratio were too high relative to a particular

"critical" value, the universe would have collapsed long ago; had it had been too low, no galaxies or stars would have formed. The initial expansion speed seems to have been finely tuned.

o Measuring the fourth number, λ (lambda), was the biggest scientific news of 1998. An unsuspected new force -a cosmic 'antigravity' controls the expansion of our universe, even though it has no discernible effect on scaled less than a billion light years. It is destined to become ever more dominant over gravity and other forces as our universe becomes ever darker and emptier. Fortunately for us (and very surprisingly to theorists), λ is very small. Otherwise its effect would have stopped galaxies and stars from forming, and cosmic evolution would have been stifled before it could have even begun.

o The seeds of all cosmic structures- stars, galaxies, and clusters of galaxies--were all imprinted in the Big Bang. The fabric of our universe depends on one number, **Q**. which represents the ratio of the two fundamental energies and is about 1/1,00,000 in value. If **Q** were much larger, it would be a violent place, in which no stars, or solar systems could survive, dominated by vast black holes.

o The sixth crucial number has been known for centuries, although it's now viewed in a new perspective. It is the number of spatial dimensions in our world, **D**, and equals three. Life couldn't exist if **D** were two or four. Time is a fourth dimension, but distinctively different from the others in that it has a built-in arrow: we 'move' only towards the future. Near black holes, space is so warped that light moves in circles, and time can stand still. [20]

Rees goes on to say that "these six numbers constitute a 'recipe' for a universe. Moreover, the outcome is sensitive to their values: if any one of them were to be 'untuned', there would be no stars and no life. Is this

---

[20] Martin Rees, *Just Six Numbers, The Deep Forces that Shape the Universe*. (New York: Basic Books, 2000) 2-3.

tuning, he asks, just a brute fact, a coincidence? Or is it the providence of a benign creator?"[21]

Physicist Stephen Barr provides a longer list of such unexplained Anthropic coincidences three of which I will discuss below:[22]

- <u>The Three Alpha Process</u>
  This relates the energy level of carbon. If the energy level of carbon-12 were different by only a small percent the synthesis of any carbon in the stars would have been extremely low-almost zero. Life is based on carbon and without large amounts of carbon, life could not occur.
- <u>The Stability of the Proton</u>
  Unlike the neutron which will decay into the proton, because it has slightly more energy, if the situation were reversed, and the proton decayed into the neutron, then not even hydrogen could exist. The difference in energy is infinitesimally small and no one knows why that should be.
- <u>The Cosmological Constant</u>
  The Cosmological Constant tells how much gravitational pull is exerted by empty space. It is an incredibly small number as a percent of the Newtonian gravitational constant, when expressed as a unitary number 1.0, it is as small as: 0.000000000000000000000000000000000000000000000000000000000001%. No one knows why it is so small, but if it were a different size, or negative, the universe after the Big Bang would have lasted only a tiny fraction of a second.

Barr continues with eight other Anthropic physical coincidences of increasing technical complexity each one of which is highly improbable, making it nearly impossible for the whole group to have occurred without some teleological direction.

---

[21] Ibid., 4.
[22] Stephen M. Barr. *Modern Physics and Ancient Faith.* (Notre Dame: University of Notre Dame Press, 2003) D

Another, and equally interesting argument for a finely tuned universe and for the Anthropic Principle is identified by Roger Penrose, who along with the late Stephen Hawking, his co-author on work concerning dark matter and black holes, is widely considered among the most accomplished mathematical physicists of our era. Penrose asserts that the only possible avenue for the development of the universe as we now know it, and for the existence of life as it is today, is the necessary requirement for an initial condition at the instant of the Big Bang of a smoothed-out state of low entropy.[23] An initial state of low entropy leading to a continuous state of low entropy as prevails now, 13.7 billion years after the singularity of the Big Bang, is an impossibility because entropy is a continuous and fundamental property of matter which runs in only one direction. However, absent this initial condition, it would be highly improbable that the low entropy state now necessary for creation and continuing existence of life, to prevail as we know it does. Penrose calculates the improbability at 10^{124} This is truly a tiny number considering that the total number of molecules in the entire universe is thought to be 10^{80}. So, what can explain this violation of the 2nd Law of Thermodynamics? Penrose admits he has no answer except to say: "The absurdly lopsided nature…must have come about from a totally different, and much deeper, reason.[24]

Does God Exist: Further Thoughts on the Proofs

These two ideas: The theories of the Big Bang and the Anthropic Principle bring us right to the threshold of certainty in the belief that God exists and that he created the universe *ex nihilo*. They do not prove the existence of God. They simply strengthen the argument. And that

---

[23] Low entropy is a well-organized condition of high available energy. High entropy is a disordered state of low or no available energy. The sun generating all the energy it does, is in a state of low entropy, however, when it exhausts all its fuel and falls apart, it will be in a state of high entropy. All physical things are subject to entropy. This is the heart of the 2nd Law of Thermodynamics

[24] Roger Penrose. *Fashion Faith and Fantasy in the New Physics of the Universe*. (Princeton: Princeton University Press, 2016). 294-323.

may be as close as we humans can expect to get, given the ontological disparity between the Creator and his creation. However, for some, this may be enough. The 19th century Catholic Cardinal, John Henry Newman, in describing his own lengthy tortured road to conversion from the Anglicanism to Catholicism, insists that certainty in such matters can be achieved only through the accumulated weight of probabilities. He says: "that absolute certitude which we were able to possess, whether as to the truths of natural theology, or as to the fact of revelation, was the result of an *assemblage* of concurring and converging probabilities..." [25] And that, I think, is the best we can hope for: an "assemblage of concurring and converging probabilities." This is an inferential method which is not only the fundamental reasoning process used by science in developing its most successful hypotheses, but also, as we have just seen, a process that can build the case for a smaller leap of faith as just about anything, yet unproven by experimentation, that science itself, would routinely have us believe.

Therefore, it should not be difficult for any person even remotely familiar with scientific reasoning to understand that the probabilities surrounding the Big Bang theory and the Anthropic Principle are so strong, that to disbelieve in God[26] is almost equivalent to disbelieving in the scientific method itself.[27]

---

[25] John Henry Newman. *Apologia Pro Vita Sua*. Ed. Ian Ker. (London: Penguin Books, 2004) 38.

[26] The Creator God as used here is a generic creator, and not necessarily the God of Christianity or any other religion.

[27] Currently, the entire system of scientific reasoning supporting the Global Climate Change hypothesis is exactly as described in this paragraph. This implies that if you accept the Climate Change hypothesis, then you should accept the existence of a creator God.

IV

Original Sin, Evolution, and The Fine Tuned Universe

The whole Adam and Eve story in the Book of Genesis has always seemed bizarre to me, and what was even more bizarre about the entire myth is that the sin of one man was said to infect with guilt, the billions of humans who would follow him in the future.[28] Ever since I was a child I thought a literal reading of this story was unacceptable. The idea of a mythical paradise, and notion that everyone is descended from a single person is believable only if one suspends one's faculty of reason. Contemporary anthropology, paleontology and archeology make short work of this illusion. This is not to say that the essence of the story is not true. I happen to think it is absolutely true; and that while a literal reading of the myth was appropriate to the state of learning prior to the advent of modern biological and genetic science, it is now possible to find theologians who are blazing new paths of interpretation. One such individual was Teilhard de Chardin, the French paleontologist and Jesuit priest, whose writings were suppressed during his lifetime. I will return to Teilhard at a later point in this essay, but at this point, I would like to provide extracts from a rather lengthy statement by Daryl P. Domning, a paleontologist and evolutionary biologist on the

---

[28] There is strong evidence that the notion of collective guilt for Adam's transgression was the result of a mistranslation. Please see pages 36-37 for more on this.

medical faculty of Howard University. In this piece, he sets forth an interpretation of the Adam and Eve story wholly consistent with the Theory of Evolution. Here is an extract from Domning's 2001 essay in America Magazine:

> ...Yet I wish to suggest that the failure of saints and scholars to solve the problem of evils has not been due to insufficient plumbing of the depths of suffering, nor to inadequate insight into the mind of God. It has resulted from our simple lack, *until the present generation*, of certain facts about how the natural world works.
>
> First is the study of animal behavior. Up through the mid-20th century, the knowledge of this subject available to philosophers and theologians hardly surpassed in depth or accuracy what we read in *Aesop's Fables*. Only in the last 30 years, thanks to workers like Jane Goodall, Dian Fossey...and many others have we gained solid, meticulously documented, quantitative knowledge of how animals (especially our closest primate relatives) really act in the wild and among themselves.
>
> The picture is not pretty. From ants to apes, the animal world is awash in intraspecific (intra-species) aggression, deceit, theft, exploitation, infanticide and cannibalism. Our cousins, the great apes are adept at political intrigue and quite capable of serial murder and lethal warfare.... The inescapable fact is that there is virtually no known human behavior that we call "sin" that is not found among non-human animals. Even pride, proverbially the deadliest sin of all, is not absent. This is not to say that these animals are guilty of sin; they are simply doing things that would be sinful if done by morally reflective human beings,,,,
>
> These revelations lead at once to an unambiguous conclusion. Logical parsimony and the formal methods of inference used in modern studies of biological

diversity affirm that these matters of behavior are displayed in common by humans and other animals *because they have been inherited from a common ancestor* which also possessed them. In biologist's jargon, they are homologous. Needless to say, this common ancestor long predated the first human and cannot be identified with the biblical Adam.

Furthermore, it is demonstrable by experiment and fully in accord with Darwinian theory that these behaviors exist because they promote the survival and reproduction of those individuals that perform them. Having once originated (ultimately through mutation), they persist because they are favored by natural selection for survival in the organism's natural environments. Since these behaviors are directed to self-perpetuation and succeed in a world of finite resources only at the expense of others, it is accurate to call them, in an entirely objective, non-psychological and non-pejorative sense, selfish. Natural selection enforces selfish behavior as the price of survival and self-perpetuation in all living things, even the simplest imaginable…

Original Sin Seen Anew

The juxtaposition of these firmly established scientific facts suggest a way to reformulate the doctrine of original sin in evolutionary terms. Original sin has been defined as *the need for salvation by Christ that is universal to all human beings and acquired through natural generation.* Descent of all human beings through a single couple-monogenism-is not essential to the doctrine; the Catholic magisterium has continued to insist on it simply in order to explain why *all* humans need to be saved. The requirement of natural generation likewise sought only to account for the undeniable fact that the tendency to sin is present in all of us, even prior to our first moral choices. It does not imply, in Augustinian fashion, that sexuality is somehow the root of all evil.

The geneticist F. J. Ayala has demonstrated (Science, 1995) that the genetic diversity of the present human population (much of which we inherit from pre-human ancestors) could not possibly have funneled through a single human couple, so monogenism must be rejected on scientific grounds alone. In any case, the requirements of the definition of original sin given above can instead be met within an evolutionary framework by distinguishing and decoupling the source of original sin's universality from the source of its moral character. these need not stem (as always has been tacitly assumed) from one and the same individual act and moment over time (the "Fall of Adam"). The overt selfish acts that, in humans, demonstrate the reality of original sin by manifesting it as actually sin do indeed owe their universality among humans to natural descent from a common ancestor. However, this ancestor must be placed not at the origin of the human race but at the origin of life itself. Yet these overt acts did not acquire their sinful character until the evolution of human intelligence allowed them to be performed by morally responsible human beings.

We all sin because we all have inherited-from the very first living things on earth-a powerful tendency to act selfishly, no matter what the cost to others. Free will allows us to override this tendency, but only sporadically and with great effort; we more readily opt for self. This tendency all of us is what tradition calls "the stain of original sin." It is not the result of a "Fall" in our prehistory, since we were never more selfless than we are now. It is present even in infants, who are undeniably self-centered, though guiltless of actually sin. We incur guilt only when we freely choose to act on this tendency to the detriment of others. Not all self-centered acts are sinful, but all sins are instances of selfishness.[29]

In this presentation, we see original sin defined as the sole and fundamental driving force essential in the nature of every living thing to always act selfishly so as to effectuate survival, adaptation, and reproduction. It is the single primordial tendency of life, but it is tendency and not an act, so calling it a sin can be correct only "in an analogical sense: it is a sin 'contracted' and not 'committed'- a state and not an act."[30] This is because for a person to commit a sin is for the person to do something; or said differently a sin is not a passive inclination, it is an act, and more specifically a freely chosen act. Thus, the commonly held assertion that we are all guilty of Adam's original sin is, if nothing else, impossibly curious.

However, as put so well by the Catholic mystic Adrienne von Speyr, "The original sin living or active within us gives each of us the predisposition to, facility for, and tendency toward actual sin"[31] In common with every other living thing, our entire physical being, as a member of the species *homo sapiens,* is permeated from birth until death by the unremitting, genetically imposed, desire to act selfishly. And were it not for the presence in humans of an intellect unique among all other forms of life, we would always act in accordance with our Darwinian tendency towards self-interest, and we would do so irrespective of the harm it might do to other things, living and non-living. However, we do have an intellect, and we do have the ability to make judgements, and we do, therefore, possess free will. Our actions, while always influenced by our inherent selfishness, are ultimately a product of our free choice and thus become moral or immoral.

---

[29] Daryl P. Domning. *Evolution, Evil and Original Sin.* America Magazine, November 12, 2001.
[30] *Catechism of the Catholic Church.* (United States Catholic Conference:1994) 404.
[31] Adrienne von Speyr, *Confession,* second Edition, Translated by Douglas W. Stott, (San Francisco: Ignatius Press, 2017),111.

So, what then is a moral act? Well, it seems to me that consistent with the naturalistic theism outlined by Domning, the starting point is that a moral act is one in which both the rational and animal principals are combined, but with the rational part prevailing. In that way, we would act in conformity with our nature as a rational animal. On the other hand, an immoral act might be one in which the rational is either absent or of negligible influence allowing our selfish nature to dominate. So, to act morally is to act rationally. But if this is a starting point, is it really enough? I don't think so.

Perhaps bringing in Aristotle's definition that man is a political (or social) animal will take us a bit further. In this calculation, man's rationality is best expressed in conforming to his political nature, thus if a person achieves his highest conformity with his nature, not in isolation, but rather in association or cooperation with others, then the moral act must not only be rational, but also must be protective of one's real or potential association with other humans.

But, if, as was discussed above, we are created by God who set in place the Darwinian logarithm of increasing biological complexity through natural selection ultimately producing the species *Homo Sapiens,* do we not owe to God, gratitude or at least some form of acknowledgement of our utter dependence to Him? It seems to me that the highest and most moral exercise of what amounts to our God-given rationality is to act, not only to protect our relationship with other humans, but also to acknowledge in gratitude our debt to God through some outward form of action.

All these things I have just mentioned: (a) acting rationally, (b) acting rationally with appreciation and care for our fellow humans, and God's creation, and (c) acting rationally in gratitude to our ultimate creator, can occur only under conditions where we consciously demand the total exclusion of our Darwinian tendency towards selfishness.

And isn't this the unalterable essence of the message of Jesus?

> And one of the scribes, approaching, hearing them debating and perceiving that he answered them well, asked him, "Which commandment is first among all?"

> Jesus answered: *"The first is: Hear, Israel the Lord our God is one Lord, And you shall love the Lord your God out of your whole heart and of your whole soul and out of your whole reason and out of your whole strength. The second is this: You shall love your neighbor as yourself. There is not another commandment greater than these."*
> Mark 12:28-31[32]

So it would seem that the truth of science is consistent with the truths of the Gospel. But there's more. The requirement that one overcome the inbred genetically instinctual propensity towards selfishness is not an easy thing to do. First a person must recognize that this instinctual behavior exists in himself and that it constitutes a serious moral weakness to which he is constantly held captive. Second, that same person, having acknowledged that the problem is within himself, must take relentless action to overcome it in all conditions. This too, is not easy. But if the matter were self-evident, and, if the impairment were easy to correct, what need would there be for the Incarnation? Consider the never-ending, pulsating, incessant and habitual urge, hard-wired from birth in every human being, to respond automatically and without thought, to nearly all inter-personal encounters, in a manner dictated by one's genetically imposed instinct towards selfishness. This indeed is a powerful force for evil present in all of us.

Yet, the Gospel tells us we must, as a matter of first and exclusive priority, do the opposite of what our nature demands. Our initial, and, automatic, non-reflective, habitual response to any personal encounter, must be not in our own interest, but rather solely in the interest of the other(s). We must go against our nature.

Jesus commands that "…you should love God out of your whole heart…your whole soul…your whole reason and out of your whole

---

[32] I have chosen to use the new translation of the New Testament by David Bentley Hart which he describes as "reconstructive" and "almost pitilessly literal."
The New Testament, translated by David Bentley Hart (New Haven: Yale University Press, 2017), Mark 12:38-31. See also, Mathew 22:35-40, Luke 10:25-28, and John 13:30-36.

strength." Yet if my assertion of the incomprehensibility of God is scripturally correct, then how can one be expected to love what is unknowable? Well, obviously the rational, analytical mode of thought is of no help, but, perhaps the intuitive, poetic or mystical mode provides the answer. Recall that earlier in this paper, I referenced Dante's description of the Trinity. This is a good example of inspired poetic knowledge. Similarly, the insights of John Milton, discussed later in this paper, regarding the nature of Satanic evil, while having only a peripheral source in scripture, may be seen also, as a possible intuitive expression of the otherwise impenetrable divine plan.

Another example of an intuitive and direct approach to God is provided by Meister Ekhart,(1260-1328), a medieval mystic who taught from his own personal experience, that every person has within himself a "divine spark" that can be accessed, but only by abnegation and completely emptying oneself to make room for God. He calls for an annihilation of self, leading to a state described as follows:

> All your activity must cease and all your powers must serve (God's) ends, not your own...No creaturely skill, nor your own wisdom, nor all your knowledge can enable you to know God divinely. For you to know God in God's way, <u>your knowing must become a pure unknowing</u>, and a forgetting of yourself and all creatures."[33]
>
> The Word lies hidden in the soul, unnoticed and unheard unless room is made for it in the ground of hearing, otherwise it is not heard; but all voices and all sounds must cease, and perfect stillness must reign there, a still silence.[34]

To love the incomprehensible God is the command. Ekhart's way is to approach a mystical union, and knowledge of God, and thus love

---

[33] Meister Ekhart quoted in, Joel F. Harrington, *Dangerous Mystic, Meister Ekhart's Path to the God Within*. (New York: Penguin Press, 2018), 238.

[34] Ibid., 241.

of God, through self-annihilation. Not everyone can attain this level of perfection, but, as Ekhart preached to his fellow Dominicans, and to the general public as well, all must try.

The second command, "to love your neighbor as yourself," seems well within the capacity of all men. However, it too, is not easy. Walter Conn, a Catholic theologian contrasts the notion of self-annihilation achieved through "denial, renunciation, abnegation..." as "standing in total opposition" to a drive for self-transcendence, also achieved through a sacrifice oriented, not to the pursuit of God from within, but rather to the pursuit of God from without, through the "denial of all those (otherwise perhaps quite legitimate) desires, wishes and interests of the self which interfere with the single-minded commitment to follow Jesus in love."[35]

While the mystic, Meister Ekhart, strives to find the spark of the divine within himself which leads to an intuitive form of comprehension of God, thus enabling the love God "with his whole heart," Conn's synthesis seems to suggest that we can approach the love of the *incomprehensible* God through the love and service of his *comprehensible* creation- man. But this, he says, requires that one move beyond one's own self through a "radical conversion of...conscience (which) finds its fullest realization in loving compassion—the self-transcending perfection of human empathy and justice."[36] Thus the unconditioned surrender of self, directed towards "single-minded commitment" to loving service of others, is the path to fulfilling the fundamental two-part Gospel command to love God, and to love one's neighbor as oneself.

But where does that leave the doctrine of the redemption? To start the discussion of this matter, I turn again to John Haught:

> Science has now demonstrated that there have been millions of years of struggle and suffering in life prior to our own emergence as a distinct species.

---

[35] Walter Conn. *Christian Conversion, A Developmental Interpretation of Autonomy and Surrender*, (New York: Paulist Press, 1986). 21,22.

[36] Ibid., 268.

This fact, it seems to me, raises significant questions about the one-sidedly anthropocentric focus of classical theology's treatment of suffering...Any theodicy that remains oblivious to the pre-human evolutionary trail of striving, pain, disease, predation, and extinction is leaving out something essential to a theologically rich understanding of God, creation and redemption...

Above all, this will mean that the theme of expiation, where guilt must be paid for by suffering, cannot plausibly function any longer as the foundation of theodicy... When Christians look for meaning in suffering, they are still under the spell of ancient mythic theodicies that interpreted suffering as the outcome of free human acts of rebellion, beginning with the spoiling of an original cosmic perfection.

In the wake of Darwin and contemporary cosmology, it is difficult...to conceive of any time in the past when the cosmos had attained perfection. Logically speaking, then, the cosmos would have been imperfect from the beginning. There always would have been a dark side to the cosmos. Consequently, no loss of primordial perfection could ever have occurred, and thus any reason to expiate an imagined transgression would be ruled out.[37]

In this passage, Haught implicitly dismisses the whole idea of a geographic and historical place in time called Paradise, in favor of a broad allegorical reading.[38] He also dismisses the idea of one man

---

[37] John F. Haught. "Teilhard and the Question of Life's Suffering." in *Rediscovering Teilhard's Fire*, ed. Kathleen Duffy S.S.J. (Philadelphia: Saint Joseph University Press, 2010) 60-61.

[38] In my view, the reconciliation of the Paradise story with the reality of evolution, can be achieved only by following the logical inferences of evolutionary science, which inexorably leads to the conclusion that the biblical drama could have occurred only in the pleroma.

committing a single transgression and thereby condemning billions of people to suffering, death and perdition, which also requires every one of these billions of people to atone or make expiation, and beg forgiveness for sin none of them had anything to do with.

Haught's reasoning is that science (and the plain common sense of observation) clearly demonstrates that the universe - God's creation - is unfinished business. It was never perfect in the beginning. Thus, he says, "the logic of evolution has now permanently closed off the path of restoration and expiation"[39] We now know that we live in a world of physical and biological evolution. The universe, 13.7 billion years ago, came from a tiny singularity of pure energy, it has not stopped evolving, and the process continues, but where it is going we do not know.

However, what we do know is that the evolutionary process is continuous, and yet, there is a necessary intervention we call the Incarnation. It is indispensable, not as an act of expiation for original sin, but rather as both a powerful, unambiguous and historically unique message from God delivered directly to humankind describing the ultimate end of the divine process, and instructing mankind how to manage its way to participate in its fruition. And as to the crucifixion itself? It is perfectly clear, especially from the First Letter of John, that Jesus was sent and sacrificed as atonement (or expiation) for our sins. But what sins?

Specifically, they are the sins that we ourselves, along with all of mankind, commit through our own volition. Unlike the guilt following upon the sin of Adam, which is an attributed guilt, and therefore no guilt at all, the guilt we incur by freely chosen sinful acts, is ours alone. And thus, it might be said that the offense we give to God by our defiance, can be absolved only by a sacrifice of equal magnitude; which is to say that offense to God must be corrected through an atonement by God. By this reasoning, the expiation is completed by the Crucifixion.

Recall that I maintain that the unbridgeable ontological chasm between God and man, makes it impossible for us to know anything at all about the nature of God. Yet we know that God appeared amongst

---

[39] Ibid., 63

us in the Incarnation and allowed himself to be subject to all the degradations of human life including suffering and death. If we think about this in terms of the ontological disparity, and express it in human terms, we are tempted to say that the Incarnation represents an act of unimaginable humility and, of incomprehensible love.

Yet, why would God do this? My answer is that we do not know and never will know. It is an unverifiable presumption to think otherwise because God is incomprehensible.

Evolution, Original Sin, The Fine-Tuned Universe: Teilhard de Chardin

Over time, God has gifted some few individuals with the attribute of prophesy to provide guidance to humankind appropriate to its then state of intellectual development. The Old Testament, for example, is replete with such lessons understandable by illiterate, semi-nomadic people, that but a few centuries later appeared artless and even ignoble, and only then made intelligible by tortured exegesis. Today, however, it may be that such a prophet has again arisen. One who has taken the advancements in science as it has approached the truth, and begun to show the way to reinterpret the Divine message in the light of such truths. I am referring, of course, to Pierre Teilhard de Chardin, who if not a prophet (which I admit is dubious), will surely be acknowledged in the future, as one of the inspired Doctors of the Church.

Teilhard's great contribution was to recognize the truth of evolution, and through an extraordinary leap of intuition, describe how the evolutionary process is the physical embodiment, not only of God's plan, but also His continuous creation of the yet unfinished universe. Emphasizing the centrality of evolution in a way that seems to put Darwin on the same paradigm shifting pedestal as Copernicus, Teilhard makes the following statement:

> "Is evolution a theory, a system or a hypothesis? It is much more: it is general condition which all

theories, all systems must bow and which they must satisfy henceforward if they are to be thinkable and true. <u>Evolution is a light illuminating all facts, a curve that all lines must follow.</u>"[40] (underlining mine)

In making this assertion, he leads us to the unavoidable conclusion that with the entire sweep of history since the singularity of the Big Bang being a movement of uninterrupted physical and biological progression from simplicity to complexity, there is a direction in which all creation is headed. He calls it the Omega Point.[41]

In Teilhard's most well-known book *The Phenomenon of Man*, the first two thirds of the text is devoted to a technical explanation of the theory of evolution. In the last third, he develops the teleological implications of evolution for which he is best known. The following paragraphs represent an attempt to stitch together a string of quotations that I hope will fairly represent his logic, although especially in this case, because I have mostly left out the spiritual component, there really is no substitute for reading the book. Here is Teilhard speaking for himself:

> Man is not the centre of the universe as we thought in our simplicity, but something more wonderful—the arrow pointing the way to the final unification of the world in terms of life. Man, alone constitutes the last born, the freshest, the most complicated, the most subtle of all the successive layers of life.[42]
>
> First the molecules of carbon compounds with their thousands of atoms symmetrically grouped; next the cell, which at the very smallest, contains thousands

---

[40] Pierre Teilhard de Chardin, *The Phenomenon of Man*, translated by Bernard Wall, (New York: Harper and Brothers Publishers, 1959), 218.

[41] In reading Theilhard, one should be aware that he uses the term "evolution" in the broadest possible way to encompass all creation moving from simplicity to complexity to its final cause. Even in the biosphere, his thought is not limited by the Darwinian thesis, but can include also, such things as genetic drift and epigenetics.

[42] Teilhard.,223.

of molecules linked in a complicated system; then the metazoan, in which the cell is no more than an infinitesimal element; and later the manifold attempts to enter into symbiosis and raise themselves to a higher biological condition. And now, as a germination of planetary dimensions, comes the thinking layer which to its full extent develops and intertwines its fibres, not to confuse or neutralize them but to reinforce them in the living unity of a single tissue. Really, I can see no coherent, and therefore scientific, way of grouping this immense succession of facts but as a gigantic psycho-biological operation, a sort of mega-synthesis, the 'super arrangement' to which all thinking elements find themselves today individually and collectively subject. Mega-synthesis in the tangential, and therefor and thereby a leap forward of the radial energies along the principal axis of evolution; ever more complexity and thus evermore consciousness.[43]

In spite of all evidence to the contrary, mankind may very well be advancing all around us at the moment... but, if it is doing so, it must be—as is the way with very big things-doing so almost imperceptibly.[44]

We have seen and admit that evolution is an ascent towards consciousness...Therefor it should culminate forwards in some sort of supreme consciousness. But must not that consciousness, if it is to be supreme, contain in the highest degree what is the perfection of our consciousness—the illuminating involution of the being upon itself?[45]

Accordingly, its enormous layers, followed in the right direction, must somewhere become involuted to

---

[43] Teilhard.,224.
[44] Teilhard.,255.
[45] Teilhard.,258.

a point which we might call *Omega*, which fuses and consumes them integrally in itself. However immense the world may be, it only exists and is finally perceptible in the directions in which its radii meet-even if this were beyond space and time altogether.[46]

Of course, the point where the world's radii meet is the *Omega*. Later, in the epilogue of *The Phenomenon of Man*, Teilhard identifies the *Omega* with God, or more specifically with the person of Christ. And this pulls his whole theological system together. In a theodicy so constructed, the natural evil of human mortality and even the sickness and disease to which all humans are subject, is essential to the completion of the vast sweep of the evolutionary direction that will ultimately culminate in Christ, the *Omega*. For Teilhard, this is the creative process of concentrating increasing layers of complexity that ultimately will resolve itself in union with the Creator who designed and set it all in motion. In the words of the Anglican clergyman Charles Kingsley, upon first reading Darwin's *Origin*: "We always knew God was wise, but He was even wiser than we thought, to make a world that could create itself."[47]

With this background, we have come to the place where we now can say that our theodicy divides Evil into two categories. The first is natural evil which is the necessary by-product of an evolutionary process that is directed like an arrow to the final merger of all creation with Christ, its creator. The second is moral evil, which is an extension of natural evil, yet is something entirely different. It occurs by freely yielding to the incessant pressure of excessive Darwinian selfishness; that encapsulates the notion of original sin, and is a powerful genetically based mindless inclination towards sin. The fact that this tendency is deeply embedded in our nature as its primary driving force is no excuse. Our obligation, as the Incarnate Jesus makes perfectly clear, is to love

---

[46] Teilhard.,259.
[47] Quoted in: Owen Gingerich. *God's Planet*,.(Cambridge: Harvard University Press, 2014). 144.

God and love our fellow humans. Violation of that rule, and everything that such violation implies, is moral evil.

Therefore, while God may be implicated in natural evil for reasons which we only vaguely understand; and for reasons that, given our ontological incompatibility, we can never expect to fully understand, when it comes to moral evil, we can blame only ourselves.

V

Comparison of this Theodicy with Selected Historical Treatments

In this section, I will be looking for philosophical and literary support for, or disagreement with, the opinions put forth in this paper. Much to my surprise, I found considerably more support than I had first expected. I also found different avenues to addressing the dilemma of evil subsisting in a supposedly good world. In *Job,* I found confirmation of my opinion that God is unknowable. In the *Summa,* I found Aquinas in agreement that the only incontrovertible source of knowledge about God is Scripture, while the authority of the Doctors of the Church, (and by implication, the Councils), is merely probable and thus subject to revision. On the other hand, I am in disagreement with his argument that the definition of evil is the absence of being; but generally comfortable with the logical process in his Argument from Design. In *Paradise Lost,* I found a more complete treatment of the "War in Heaven" and the nature of Satan than is available in Scripture. I also found in Milton, a gateway to a discussion of Satanic Evil, and the supernatural source of such evil called Satan, who because he is not empirically verifiable has been thus far absent from my theodicy. However, inasmuch as that absence is a substantial defect, it is repaired in the section on John Milton's *Paradise Lost.* In David Hume's *Dialogues Concerning Natural Religion,* I found a nice division of evil into two parts; Natural and

Moral that followed the same lines as my own analysis. I also found an intriguing observation that God is morally neutral; and, interestingly, he also seems to consider God to be unknowable, and therefore we cannot know he reconciles the problem of evil. Voltaire's *Candide* leaves little doubt that that we do not live in the best of all possible worlds as he chronicles a vast catalogue of moral evil. Finally, Camus' *The Plague*, provides a marvelous opportunity to reflect on the place of natural evil in the overall landscape of evolution.

The Book of Job.

This text is probably the most unlikely, difficult to understand of any book of the Old Testament. God is portrayed as willful, capricious and uncaring. Satan appears almost as his equal. Their bargain is cruel and mean spirited as they victimize Job, and destroy his life for their own entertainment. What possibly could be the purpose of such a tale? Simply to prove that one human, in the face of terrible evil, still remains faithful to God? Perhaps, but that is only part of the story. Much more important, it seems to me is the message that the ways of God are different from the ways of man. This is an extended allegory with a single purpose, and that is to demonstrate that God is unknowable and our attempts to assign human characteristics to Him are impossible. At the end of the poem we hear this lesson clearly, when God says to a still proud and angry Job, "Who is this who darkens counsel in words without knowledge?" In other words, 'you know nothing about Me.' Then God goes on to say, sarcastically, "Where were you when I founded the earth?" This is followed by the two penultimate verses in which God catalogues His greatness and by implication, Job's (man's) insignificance and absolute ignorance regarding God and his motives. This, for me, affirms the view that the ontological disparity between God and humankind rules out any possibility of our knowing anything at all about God, His nature, and His motives.

Thomas Aquinas on Scriptural vs. Philosophical Authority.

I am always pleasantly surprised when I pick up the *Summa,* or other works by Thomas Aquinas because of the universality of his insights; and this, also to my surprise, is despitehis ubiquitous references to metaphysical concepts which in most cases, I view as an impediment to his otherwise brilliant logic.

Earlier, when discussing the Trinity, I tried to make the case (along with Pope Benedict XVI) that the words used for the formulation of the doctrine of the Trinity were inadequate to the subject. Moreover, by extension, I suggested that one might see that other traditional formulations of Catholic doctrine may well be equally inadequate. Some of them could do with revision or, at least updating, to accommodate the advancement of general knowledge that have occurred since the 4th or 5th century when much of this doctrine was set in stone. Of course, this is not very likely.[48]

However, I found that Aquinas seems to be in agreement with my opinion, as follows:

> ...natural reason should minister to faith as the natural bent of the will ministers to charity...Hence sacred doctrine makes use also of the authority of philosophers in these questions in which they were able to know the truth by natural reason.., sacred doctrine makes use of these authorities as extrinsic and probable arguments; but properly uses the authority of the canonical Scriptures as an incontrovertible proof, and the authority of the doctors of the Church as one may properly be used, yet merely as probable. For our

---

[48] That the magisterium of the church is unlikely to consider any revision or updating of doctrine is based on my opinion that the hierarchy operates on the principal of fear. A fear that any changes will confuse the faithful and cause defections. Of course, they never think that the <u>failure</u> to make such changes may have or will cause an even greater number to leave the Church.

faith rests upon the revelation made to the apostles and prophets, who wrote the canonical books, and not on the revelations (if any such there are) made to other doctors.[49]

So, if I understand this correctly, revelation and the prophets are the only absolute authority; everything else, even the pronouncements of Church Councils, is contingent, and since classified as "probable," it is subject to change. Therefore, he would appear to be in sympathy with the position that there is no reason why contemporary science should be excluded from use as a vehicle to interpret Scripture.

Now, before going further with the discussion of Aquinas, I would like to introduce a complementary piece of information that might shed some light on the uncertainty of one important teaching of the Church. For this I will turn to a footnote in the David Bentley Hart translation of the New Testament. This note refers to what Hart identifies as a mistranslation by Jerome of the passage in Paul's Letter to The Romans, Paul 5:12. Regarding this passage he says:

> A fairly easy verse to follow until one reaches the final four words, whose precise meaning is already obscure, and whose notoriously defective rendering in the Latin Vulgate ...constitutes one of the most consequential mistranslations in Christian history.[50]

There follows a lengthy technical analysis of the original Greek, and then he says:

> Hence what became the standard reading of the verse in much of Western theology after the late third

---

[49] Thomas Aquinas, "Summa Theologica 1.1,8.", in Peter Kreeft, Ed. *Summa of the Summa*, (San Francisco: Ignatius Press, 1990) 47. And in Anton C. Pegis, Ed. *Basic Writings of Saint Thomas Aquinas*, (New York: Random House, 1945) 14.

[50] The New Testament, translated by David Bentley Hart (New Haven: Yale University Press) note p, 296.

century: "in whom (i.e. Adam) all sinned." This is the *locus classicus* of the Western Christian notion of original guilt—the idea that in some sense all human beings had sinned *in* Adam, and therefore everyone is born already damnably guilty in the eyes of God—<u>a logical and moral paradox that Eastern tradition was spared by its knowledge of Greek</u>. Paul speaks of death and sin as a kind of contagion here, a disease with which all are born; and elsewhere he describes it as a condition like civil enslavement to an unjust master, from which we must be "redeemed" with a manumission fee: <u>but never as an inherited condition of criminal culpability</u>.[51] (underlining mine).

I inserted this little diversion to point out that, not only can the doctors of the Church be subject error, but even Sacred Scripture, if mistranslated, can be similarly subject to interpretative or exegetical error.

But isn't this interesting? It would seem that the interpretation of original sin proffered earlier in this paper, in which we call into question the traditional expiatory property of original sin, may not be quite so at variance with the doctrine of original sin as it first appeared in the first century Greek of Paul's epistle.[52]

That said, we now return to Aquinas.

Thomas Aquinas on Evil.

As much as I am impressed with Aquinas' teachings, I have found that not infrequently, he ties himself in knots trying to fit religious

---

[51] Ibid., 297-297.
[52] Origen appears to agree with the notion that Original Sin was <u>not</u> passed down to the human race through inherited guilt, see: Origen, Commentary on the Epistles to the Romans, Books 1-5, *in The Fathers of the Church*, translated by Thomas P. Scheck, (Washington, D.C.: The Catholic University Press, 2001), 303-328.

or scientific truths into a preconceived metaphysical framework. His definition of evil is one such example, for in the *Summa,* he defines evil as the absence of good. From the perspective of this theodicy, this definition is a dead end, because the understanding of evil as described in this paper is that it is an <u>act</u> causing harm. Aquinas, however, would see evil as <u>a state of being</u> in a static universe, the cause of the evil act being some defect on the agent. On the other hand, he is loose with his use of the term evil. For example, he calls blindness an evil. Well, that is just plain wrong.

Blindness is a condition or a disorder. It is certainly a defect from the so-called "good," but it is not an act, it is a state of being which could have been caused by a defect in the conceptual or birthing process, a sickness or disease or, on the other hand, by an act by the individual himself, or by a third party or, by an accident. Blindness, therefore, can be the consequence of evil, and only imprecisely described as evil in itself. Aquinas insists that evil is a privation of good, and certainly blindness fits that description, but what does that have to do with evil as understood as moral action or evil as understood as acts of nature, much less than, evil as caused by Satan? He later allows how the perfection of the universe requires gradations in goodness which, in turn means that some things are a mixture of being and non-being, which is plainly contradictory.[53] In, excusable ignorance, he claims that corruption is found in things.[54] Well, we know that is not true. Corruption (or the fact that things rot and deteriorate over time) is not inherent in material things. It is caused by an outside agency, that is, the action of prokaryotes. Absent prokaryotic action, there is no "corruption" found in things.

Thomas Aquinas on the Proof of God's Existence by Intelligent Design.

Aquinas does not fall into the trap of attributing the marvelous construction of living things, like humans (for example), to God's

---
[53] *Summa,* I.49, 1-2.
[54] *Summa,* I.48,2.

specific design, as is common with most intelligent design advocates right up to, and including our own present day. His argument is more nuanced, and based not in the design of specific things, but rather on the process by which things come into existence. It is the process, not unlike evolution, which he with Aristotle, identifies as final causality.[55] Although, while evolution posits its movement on random undirected mutations leading to adaptation over deep time, Aquinas, would reject the seemingly random nature of the modern evolutionary theory and require an "intelligent designer" to direct the process. Nevertheless, there is nothing in evolutionary theory to exclude a long trending overarching teleological pattern analogous to a final cause; or an intelligent designer who creates a process by which evolution can work to an ultimate design-an intelligent designer who can create "a world that can create itself."

Thomas Aquinas on Man's Comprehension of God

Aquinas says that the name HE WHO IS, is most properly applied to God. He then makes the following statement with which I am certainly in agreement:

> Now our intellect cannot know the essence of God itself in this life, but whatever mode it applies in determining what it understands about God, it falls short of the mode of what God is in himself.[56]

Thomas Aquinas on the Teleological Direction of the Universe

We are in complete agreement. He says, "...the unvarying course of natural things which are without knowledge, shows clearly that the

---

[55] *Summa*, I.2,3.
[56] *Summa*. I,13,11.

world is governed by some reason." [57] Later, he describes this movement by explaining that, "...that good which is the end of the whole universe must be a good outside of the universe..." Namely God.[58]

John Milton, *Paradise Lost*.

This work presents the standard Christian doctrine on evil. This is a view that evolutionary empiricism will proscribe because it cannot be proved. Yet, there is little doubt that some eruptions of evil are so monstrous and so deeply embedded in their host cultures that they resist simple empirical analysis. Moreover, I find it an abuse of reason to assign such "eruptions" to an extension of evolutionary theory because the concept of evolution is grounded on an accumulation of many small things occurring over deep time, while the massive "eruptions" of evil are very big things occurring over a very short length of time.

Here is a list of six big 20th century horrors, each one responsible for violent deaths exceeding ten million humans:

- The First World War (1914-18)
- The Second World War (1939-45)
- The Starvation of Ukrainians and Kazakhs by Stalin (1932-33)
- The Jewish Holocaust during World War Two (1939-45)
- Mao's Great Leap Forward (1958-62)
- Worldwide Fetal Extinction by Abortion (1973—)

When scanning this list, one can discern a single thread of common motivation: each one of these "eruptions" were <u>ideologically motivated</u>. On the other hand, it must be admitted that when one considers all the nightmarish big evil events of history, it is evident that only some were ideological, like the wars of religion, while others, probably comprising the majority, were wars of conquest. Wars of conquest, I would argue,

---

[57] *Summa*, I,103,1.
[58] *Summa*, I,103,3.

may be readily comprehended within an evolutionary theodicy. But wars of ideology may not.[59]

These and similar events, it seems to me, are inexplicable, except with reference to the supernatural principal of evil we call Satan or the devil. How else, for example, can one explain the organized, industrialized extermination of six million humans involving the willing participation of tens of thousands of otherwise "respectable church going" people, except by total subversion of each of these "respectable" individual's consciences' to the point where in their own minds, the ultimate evil of killing innocent people becomes a good, moral, and correct event in which to participate. I believe this category of evil is nothing less than the effective elimination of rationality through the substitution of a debased ideology. Can such a phenomenon, which infects millions of people, occur naturally? I do not see how the evolutionary tendencies we have discussed, can be so uniformly distorted on such a wide scale. Therefore, I would suggest that moral evil can be divided into two categories: (1) Evil that is derived by the failure of reason or the distortion of the genetically imposed inclination to selfishness, and (2) Evil that is Satanic in its origin which, for lack of a better term, I call "Big Evil."

The reader might question my resorting to Satan as the source of "Big Evil." How can God have created Satan? Who is Satan? Why, in the Divine economy, does he exist? This is the 'bottom-line' question of Theodicy.

---

[59] The term "ideology" may be broadly defined as a system of ideas typically regarding social and religious matters. Historically, nearly all ideologies are more or less morally neutral. Occasionally, ideologies are taken to the extreme when their proponents insist that their system of ideas is so indisputable and that any and all opposing beliefs are in error, and in their world, error has no rights. This is an absolutist stance that, by definitions is a denial of rationality. A perfect example is the Inquisition. Other examples (from the last century) would include both the Nazi regime and Communism as practiced by Stalin and Mao. Examples from the current century are Radical Islam, ISIS, and the Late Term abortion movement. All of these have in common the characterization of their opposition as illegitimate, having no rights, and thus unworthy of freedom of speech and thought, and subject to suppression (or worse).

Up to now, we have reduced much of the appearance of evil to its evolutionary origins. However, notwithstanding the near universality of the evolutionary explanation, we are still left with a hard core of evil that defies evolutionary justification. This I attribute to Satan. The presence of Satan in the world is testified 35 times in the New Testament. These are explicit references, not those drawn from complicated exegesis or interpretation, Satan is referenced by name, leaving no doubt that, in the minds and experience of Jesus and the Holy Spirit, such a being exists.[60] But, why should God have permitted this? I have no answer, except to fall back on the notion, expressed earlier, that God, his actions, and his attributes are incomprehensible to mankind. Nevertheless, while an explanation of why Satan exists is out of reach, it seems to me that an analysis of Satanic manifestation should be possible. One of these is "Big Evil."

Biblical scholar, John Dominic Crossan, identifies various modes of what I call "Big Evil." He says:

>...I propose that human violence can move through three successive stages-from ideological, through rhetorical to physical violence, as follows:
>
>*Ideological* violence is *thinking* that persons, groups, or nations are inhuman, or at least seriously lacking in the humanity one grants oneself.
>
>*Rhetorical* violence is *speaking* on that presumption by dehumanizing those others with rude names, crude caricatures, and derogatory stereotypes or by calling them political "traitors" or religious "heretics."
>
>*Physical*- and even lethal-violence is *acting* on these presuppositions either by illegal attack or, if one has attained social power, by official, legal political action.[61]

---

[60] There are a variety of names used to describe Satan, each referring to the same entity: Satan, The devil, Beelzebub, The wicked one, The tempter, The Liar and father of lies, The god /prince/ruler of this world, Belial, The dragon, The ancient serpent.

[61] John Dominic Crossan. *The Power of Parable*, (New York: Harper-Collins Publishers, 2012), 181

If one analyzes the highlighted eruptions of "Big Evil" during the 20th century, it is very easy to see how these horrors have progressed through Crossan's three stages of violence. What is not easy to see is how this occurred, especially, how the successive three stages flowed seamlessly through a wide swath of society. Again, I have no answer except to point to Satan, the great deceiver.

Philosopher Leszek Kolakowski, a witness to the horrors of World War II and the Jewish Holocaust puts it thusly: "the devil is part of our experience. Our generation has seen enough of it for the message to be taken extremely seriously. Evil, I contend, is not contingent, it is not the absence, or deformation, or subversion of virtue (or whatever else we may think of as its opposite), but a stubborn and unredeemable fact"[62]

Central to Christian teaching is the existence of a force for evil personified by Satan and his hosts of evil spirits. He is tolerated by a supposedly all powerful God. Why? We do not know. Satan, under various names, is mentioned 35 times in the New Testament. However, for me, the most important reference to Satan is found in the last petition in the prayer taught by Jesus to his disciples-The Lord's Prayer.

The Orthodox are very clear in this matter. Their prayer ends with the petition: "Deliver us from the evil *one*." The Roman Catholics are less precise. Their prayer ends with the petition: "Deliver us from evil." I found this curious, so I went to the Gospel to see what was actually reported as the words of Jesus. The Lord's Prayer is set forth in two gospels: Mathew 6: 9-13, and Luke 11: 2-4. Here is a table showing the results for three editions:

Translation	Matthew 6: 9-13	Luke 11: 2-4
King James	Deliver us from evil	Deliver us from evil
NRSV Catholic Edition	Rescue us from the evil one	(no mention)
David Bentley Hart	Rescue us from him who is wicked	(no mention)

---

[62] Leszek Kolakowski, *My Correct Views on Everything*, ed. Zbigniew Janowski (South Bend: St. Augustine's Press, 2005), 133.

It looks to me that the committee writing the King James version deliberately watered it down, perhaps in sympathy with the Reformation's rejection of all things "Roman."

However, the Catechism of the Catholic Church, in explaining this petition, directs the reader, not only to the verses quoted above, but also, to Jesus' prayer in John 17:15. In this passage, Jesus, prior to his trial and crucifixion, praying to the Father on behalf of his disciples, says: "I am not asking you to take them out of this world, but I ask you to protect them from the evil *one*."

So, taking the weight of evidence: the translations of Matthew, the prayer of Jesus reported in John, and numerous other New Testament references, I conclude that regardless of what is in the Catholic Liturgy, the unambiguous Christian doctrine is that Satan is a person (or something analogous to a person in the spiritual domain). It is this personified reality of evil, in the creature called Satan, that is what John Milton's *Paradise Lost* is all about.

In this book, I am endeavoring to measure the selected readings within the context of a theodicy inspired by evolutionary theory as drawn out by the theological school of Teilhard de Chardin and further enlightened by the late 20th century findings of molecular biology.

Clearly, the standard narrative of the Fall does not fit into an evolutionary reading of history, for two reasons: (1) The genetically imbedded tendency to commit moral evil which is theologically called Original Sin appeared in living organisms over 3.0 billion years before the appearance of humans, so attributing this inclination to the Fall of man is a biological impossibility. (2) There is no geological, anthropological or archeological evidence to support the narrative of the Fall and the existence of Paradise as occurring on earth. That said, if one insists that the Fall was an actual event that occurred in history, there is nothing in the record (nor will there ever be) to prevent an interpretation of this events from having occurred in the pleroma at some time concurrent with, or before, the appearance of life on earth.

One of the intriguing aspects of this project to reconcile an empirically grounded evolutionary theodicy with traditional Christianity, is that once started on this trail, one becomes captive to an irresistibly relentless logic leading to unexpected outcomes. One such outcome is the discovery that the story of the Fall, if considered an historical event, could have occurred nowhere else but in the pleroma. A second, and even more surprising conclusion is that Satan is not finished; having first spoiled God's plan for a perfect world for mankind, he is now determined to continue distorting human free will, increasingly on a vast scale, in order to prevent mankind's teleological return to the Creator.

Earlier it was suggested that there are many ways of knowing. And since we are studying the nature of evil, and since the biblical references are scanty, we are fortunate in having in the work of John Milton, a creative illumination of this subject, and of Satan, its progenitor.[63]

Milton's three-part problem in dealing with Satan was how to account for his existence, how to account for his leading a "War in Heaven" in rebellion against the God the father, and how to understand the source of his evil nature. Milton solves this problem by resorting to the ancient Arian heresy, Recall, that the traditional Christian teaching says that the Father and the Son are both one in being and co-eternal. However, Arius, a priest from Alexandria, in the early 4th century taught that the son was subordinate and created in time after the father. The idea spread throughout the Roman Empire popularized among the common people by the Arian chant: "There was once when he was not." This concept of the inequality of the persons in the trinity was condemned by the First Council of Nicaea (325AD). However, while the Catholic, Orthodox, and mainline Protestant churches accept the Nicene creed and the condemnation of the Arian formula, there still remain pockets of Christianity that, even today, hold faithfully to some form of Arianism.

In Book V of *Paradise Lost*, Milton describes events in heaven with God announcing to the assembled angelic population the following: "Hear all ye angels, progeny of light...Hear my decree, which unprovoked shall stand. This day I have begot whom I declare my only

---

[63] It appears that Milton's biblical source for the "War in Heaven" was Revelation 12:6-10 which is phrased as a forecast of future events. But traditionally, many biblical scholars have also interpreted it as describing past events from which Satan emerged as God's adversary on earth.

Son, and on this holy hill him I have anointed, whom you now behold at my right hand; your head I him appoint; to him shall bow all knees in heav'n, and shall confess him Lord: united under his great vicegerent reign abide…[64]

Notice that God says "<u>This day</u> I have begot…" He is here speaking to a pre-existing assembly of angels, and, of course He himself is pre-existent. So, measuring time only by the sequence of events, it is clear that Milton adheres to the Arian formula: "There once was when he was not." However, the begetting of the Son is something like a divine mitosis, so inasmuch as the Son shares the Father's substance, one can say that he is eternal.

Nevertheless, that does not take away from the fact that the timing of the event, the begetting, occurred sequentially <u>after</u> the creation of the angels.

For Satan (whose name was different before his rebellion), the appearance of the Son presents an irredeemable challenge because prior to the begetting of the Son, Satan was preeminent among the angelic host, with not only some sort of leadership role among all the angels, but also some sort of quasi-independent barony in the "north." God's proclamation reduces Satan's status. He is publicly humiliated. Naturally, his reaction is anger, bitterness, and envy.

"Satan" Milton relates, "…fraught with envy…could not bear through pride that sight, and thought himself impaired. Deep malice thence conceiving and disdain(fully)…he resolved with all his legions to dislodge and leave unworshipped, unobeyed the throne supreme contemptuous…"[65] Satan draws about a third of the angels to his palace in the north where he sarcastically questions the Father's declaration that the angels were created by: "…the work of secondary hands, by task transferred from Father to Son? Strange point and new!" [66] Clearly, he finds to be nonsense that the begotten Son was the creator of angels who preceded him in time. Expanding on his disbelief, he then says:

---

[64] John Milton, *Paradise Lost*, ed. William Kerrigan, John Rumrich, and Stephan M. Fallon, (New York: Random House, Inc. 2007), 184-185.
[65] Ibid.,186-187.
[66] Ibid.,193.

'We know of no time when we were not as now; know none before us, self-begot, self-raised by our own quickening power..."[67] Here we can discern some of Satan's perspective. He is envious, disrespectful of God, disbelieving in the co-equality and co-eternity of the Son, and abounding in pride as to angelic power.

His pride and confidence, seconded by his equally prideful followers, takes the form of armed rebellion. The War in Heaven ebbs and flows over three days of violent battle, until Satan and his horde of rebellious angels (now devils) are finally vanquished by the Son, and thrown into the dark, fiery depths of hell.

As told by Milton, Satan is defeated, but he is not done; he escapes from hell, discovers God's new creation, mankind, who is to be a substitute for the fallen and lost angels. God places man in paradise, an environment in dramatic contrast with the horrors of hell. Stung by jealousy and seeking vengeance, Satan learns that man can be corrupted by guile, which he promptly does; thus, ruining God's plan. Moreover, he and his evil multitude set themselves up along-side now fallen mankind to continue the corruption of each subsequent generation after Adam. Satan is now engaged in eternal total war with God over the allegiance of man, and he has won a major battle in causing Adam's fall, and infecting the rest of mankind with enough temptation to jeopardize Man's redemption and ultimate return to God.

Milton has taken us beyond scripture and shown us Satan's evil nature as well as the origin of his evil nature. Milton's Satan is racked with pride, envy, vengeance, and most importantly, pure hatred for God and his creation. Milton locates the source of Satan's envy, vengeance, and hatred in God's announcement of His newly begotten Son holding equal power and authority with God the Father, thus humiliating Satan and displacing him from his former preeminence. This action was an irreconcilable affront to Satan whose pride could not be bent to acquiescence.

So, if we accept Milton's insights, and combine them with the Teilhardian teleology, then simple logic leads to the conclusion that

---

[67] Ibid.,193.

Satan's vengeful goal is to frustrate man's evolutionary return to God. And how could he do this? I would propose that his method would involve causing the human race to destroy itself, or at a minimum, interrupt evolutionary progress. And this is what I call "Big Evil." Among other things this might include wholesale thermonuclear war, or destruction of the environment, or human breeding to the level that the population exceeds the carrying capacity of the planet. None of these three mega-events is, in our day, inconceivable.

David Hume, *Dialogues Concerning Natural Religion*

Hume's *Dialogues* speak directly to the subject matter of this essay. There are three participants: Demea, who represents orthodox religion and assumes as a given, the reality of God's existence, but nevertheless, argues that we cannot know the nature of God through reason or any other way; Cleanthes, who argues that God's existence and essence can be known through the evidence of nature; and Philo, a skeptic. The *Dialogues* proceed along two branches. The first is to prove the existence of God from nature by use of the argument from intelligent design. The second is to determine the nature of God by an analysis of effects.

A principal theme in the earlier parts of my essay relates to the errors that historically arise when religion or philosophy relies on the contemporaneous state of scientific knowledge (or lack of knowledge); and the care that the reader must exercise in its interpretation. Just as much of the Old Testament was written for primitive peoples ignorant of any rational knowledge of nature, and much of Church doctrine is clothed in the language of 4th century science and philosophy, and the scholastic theology of the 12th through 14th century's is infested with meaningless Aristotelian pseudo-physics, Hume's *Dialogues* are similarly affected. Probably half of the *Dialogues* is devoted to a discussion of the old argument from design in which the origin of complex natural objects and phenomena, is held to be impossible without an intelligent designer (i.e. God). Of course, just about a century later this whole idea was rendered useless by Darwinian evolution; and what Darwin did for the life sciences, the physicists and astronomers of the 20th century did for the physical sciences. So, history's relentless advance in knowledge has made first part of Hume's *Dialogues* essentially meaningless.[68]

The second branch of his argument, the study of God by reference to his effects in nature, is an entirely different matter and not at all subject to the infirmities inherent in the reliance on contemporaneous science. In the later parts, Philo seems to be taking the lead. He asks this question: "Is he (God) willing to prevent evil, but not able? Then he is impotent. Is he able? But not willing? Then he is malevolent. Is he both able and willing? Whence then is evil?"[69] Much of the discussion concerns different causes of natural and moral evil. Philo's final conclusion is that God is morally neutral and thus indifferent; and so long as we admit that God is unknowable, and thus we do not know whether or not he shares human characteristics like compassion, justice etc., we cannot know how he reconciles the problem of evil.

Two Novels: Voltaire, *Candide*, Camus, *The Plague*

These two novels present us with descriptions of the two categories of evil. Voltaire sets forth a voluminous satire cataloguing the many varieties of moral evil. Camus provides an in-depth study of a single example of natural or physical evil.

Voltaire's satirical study of evil, apart from his description of the Lisbon earthquake and tsunami, is almost entirely centered on moral issues which he describes exceedingly well. *Candide* is the victim of human sinfulness where the events become readily understandable insofar as each individual incident aligns perfectly with the concept of Darwinian selfishness.

---

[68] Notwithstanding the certainties expressed in this paper, it must be readily admitted that the use of the Big Bang theory, the Anthropic Principal, and Darwinian evolution, may in the future be just as obsolete as was Aristotelian cosmology.

[69] David Hume. *Dialogues Concerning Natural Religion*, in "The English Philosophers from Bacon to Mill". ed. Edwin A. Burt, (New York: The Modern Library, 1939), 741.

On the other hand, Camus's *Plague* raises troubling questions regarding proportionality in the matter of natural evil. It may be recalled that in my analysis of the evolutionary cause of natural evil, such evil was justified and explained by an overarching teleological thrust of evolutionary progress working its way towards ultimate union with Christ. Minor evils are tolerated because they are disproportionately small in the context of the overall direction of life, and because in the Teilhardian theodicy, they are seen as necessary to the evolutionary process that is the means by which end is attained by all humanity.

Camus' plague is a microcosm of the pandemic of 542 in which it is estimated that 30 million people died, thus hollowing out the Eastern Roman Empire, and thereby allowing the spread of the Islamic armies of conquest. It also is comparable in severity to the European Black Death of 1347-52 in which fully one half of Europe's population was eliminated. These tragedies, as well as that in North Africa described by Camus, were caused by the bacteria *Yersinia pestis*. Why one may ask, does God allow such horrible things to exist? What possible good could they do? How do such things fit into the evolutionary tree of life? In the 20th century, we have become sadly accustomed to moral evil of such large proportion, but rarely, if ever, do other living things cause natural evil on such a scale. What is the meaning of this?

Well, first we should understand that *Yersina pestis* is a bacterium, a unicellular object and thus a member of the biological domain prokaryote, which is an organism that lacks a membrane-bound nucleus. Prokaryotes were the first living organism on earth, appearing between 3.5 to 4.2 billion years ago. Their evolutionary cousin, eukaryotes which are unicellular objects with a membrane bound-nucleus, appeared about 1.5 billion years later. It is from the prokaryote and the eukaryote that all living organisms, including plants, animals, and humans, are derived. There are today 5×10^{30} prokaryotic bacteria living on earth. They comprise a biomass larger than all other plants and animals combined. There are between 100 million and one billion bacterial cells in a gram of soil. The human body comprises about 37 trillion human cells, while there are about 39 trillion prokaryotes (bacteria) living on and within each person. Bacteria can reproduce every 10-30 minutes and will live until they have exhausted their food source. So, imagine the number of evolutionary "mutations" that have occurred every 30 minutes for 3.5 billion years.[70] This has resulted in an estimated 10^9 total species of which biologists have identified only 9,300. One of these is *Yersina pestis* which causes bubonic plague, but most are benign and many are essential for both plant and animal life. Prokaryotes (bacteria) were the first living things, but in their initial 300 million years of life on earth, bacteria subsisting in an atmosphere totally devoid of oxygen, were the sole source of all the oxygen on earth. Bacteria in the soil converts gaseous nitrogen in air to nitrogen compounds that the plants can absorb, and without which they cannot live. As for animals, including humans, bacteria in the digestive system provides the means for waste conversion and disposal. Absent such organisms, we could not process food and thus could not live.

So, in the grand sweep of evolution, bacteria have a place in that they enable higher forms of life to emerge and live, but in their own evolution, along-side the multitude of "good" bacteria, a few outliers or harmful bacteria have been mutated. *Yersina pestis* is one.[71]

Thus, in terms of evolutionary theodicy, when I read *The Plague* and consider the prokaryotic cause of the evil, I am saddened by the event just as I am saddened by the pandemics that preceded it. But, these events take on a different and somewhat less tragic meaning when put in the context of the billions and billions of human lives that comprise the entire human

---

[70] This use of the term mutation is only a shorthand way of describing prokaryotic genetic variation. Prokaryotes reproduce by Binary Fission. They simply split apart into two identical cells. Genetic variation is achieved by: (1) Transformation in which a prokaryote takes in a random piece of DNA floating in its environment, (2) Transduction, in which DNA is moved accidentally from one prokaryote to another by a virus, (3) Conjugation, in which DNA is transferred between prokaryotes through a hair-like appendage called the pilus, and (4) Transposable Elements which are pieces of DNA that can move from one place to another within the cell and are then transferred from one cell to another by transformation, transduction, or conjugation.

[71] An excellent description of the evolution and genetics of bacteria for the non-scientist, may be found in: William Rosen, *Justinian's Flea*, (New York: Viking Press, 2007), 170-197.

race since its emergence some 300 million years ago, who would never have lived at all, but for the presence of prokaryotic cousins of *Yersina pestis*.

Brian Davies, O.P., *The Reality of God and the Problem of Evil*

Brian Davies is a contemporary philosopher, having taught at Oxford and Fordham. As one might expect of a Dominican priest, he is a straight down the line Thomist. And thus, an excellent example of contemporary Thomistic theological reasoning. He is a traditionalist, and in this respect, he does not deviate in any way from the Magisterium, (the teaching authority of the Church).

Not surprisingly, he is as firm as I am in his conviction that God is in every way incomprehensible – and he holds this position, which he also attributes to Aquinas, for the same reason, because God and man are ontologically incompatible. Or said differently, if God is the creator, he has to be outside of creation.

Once we understand this most fundamental point, the question of Theodicy goes away, because God is not one of us and therefore, contrary to traditional teaching, we cannot necessarily attribute to Him human attributes or virtues. So, we logically cannot say God is good (at least not in the sense of moral good). Neither can we say that *all* evil is bad for us, because we do not know the whole story, some evil may be the means to a good end.

For example, my discussion of the plague and the role of prokaryotes in both causing sickness, while enabling the processes without which all human and higher forms of life could not exist, while never expressed by traditionalists like Davies, is certainly not inconsistent with their theology.

Summary of Findings

Up to now, we have analyzed the phenomenon of evil by dividing it into two parts: natural evil and moral evil, with moral evil being nothing more than an aberration or perverse extension of natural evil. However, at some point, this analysis fails. We reach a dead end, because some manifestations of evil, though uncommon, are so abhorrent, so contrary to even the most perverse distortion of Darwinian tendencies, that they can be explained only by the influence of an external or Satanic agent. This notion is first introduced on pages 43-48. It will be further developed in what follows.

I call this type of evil "Big Evil." The *Holocaust* is an example of "Big Evil." And in our current times, the *World-Wide Fetal Extinction by Abortion*, is its most pervasive eruption. Most of the remaining sections of this paper, starting with a discussion of the human genome (pages 57-69, and the discussion of ideology as the means by which Satan accomplishes his objectives (pages 73-76), are focused on this matter

VI

The Human Genome

Thus far, we have surveyed the theory and theological implications of evolution solely from a morphological perspective. The question remains whether this discussion can be brought down to the molecular level? In the 1930's and 40's, when Theilhard was writing, to incorporate molecular affects in his orthogenetic analysis, would have been impossible, because the science had not yet been done. But now, eighty years later, the advances in biogenetic sciences, especially those since 2003, should provide a path forward.

In 1852, Charles Darwin published *On the Origin of the Species*, which ultimately became the unifying theory of the life sciences. In 1866, Gregor Mendel, an Augustinian monk, published his *Experiments in Plant Hybridization* in an obscure journal, but it was not until 1900 that his work was "rediscovered" by the scientific community. Darwin's *"Origin"* had some fundamental problems because it lacked an explanation of the mechanism that enabled the inheritance of random variations which was the foundation upon which natural selection operated. Mendel's research provided the missing answer. The incorporation of Mendel's theories of genetic inheritance as an integral part of Darwin's overall concept of the variation of traits within a species, and of the development or origin of new species had, by the early decades of the 20th century completed the theory of evolution through natural selection. It became known as Neo-Darwinism or the Modern Synthesis.

The main elements of Neo-Darwinism are:[72]

- All changes in genetic material are random.
- Random variations in the reproductive cells (primarily mutations) produce organisms that are less or more fit in the environment they find themselves in.
- The more fit organisms produce more offspring that are fertile than the less fit ones.
- This will lead to the genes in the fitter individuals coming to dominate the gene pool of the population, This is natural selection, Darwin's central idea.
- Finally, the inheritance of acquired characteristics is impossible.

Such was the state of evolutionary science in the first half of the 20th century when Theilhard was developing his orthogenetic synthesis of religion and science. Early in the period, it was determined that forty-six chromosomes populate each human cell. The 1940's saw the beginnings of molecular biology which was eventually integrated into the Neo-Darwinian synthesis providing, by the late 1990's, a genetic and molecular explanation of evolution. A critical finding of molecular biology occurred in 1953, when Francis Crick and James Watson found that DNA, structured like two chains in the shape of a ladder-like double helix twisted into a coil configuration. It is made up of four base chemicals that can produce roughly three billion different combinations. Moreover, within each of the 46 human chromosome there resides DNA molecules which individually may contain 20,000 genes. In 1995, the human genome project was initiated for the purpose of sequencing a human DNA molecule to unlock its genetic composition.

During the second half of the 20th century, the state of biological research was intense. One can only express wonder and awe at the rapid

---

[72] This list, with some modest paraphrasing is taken from, Dennis Noble, *Dance to the Tune of Life, Biological Relativity*. (Cambridge: Cambridge University Press, 2017) 206.

progress made by researchers working within the unimaginably small scale of the physical and biological phenomena of the living cell. Their findings makes nonsense of the old fashioned explanations of nature so fondly embraced by religious and other authorities. Here is an example from today's world of genetics, describing the DNA present in each one of our 18 trillion[73] somatic cells:

> The human genome is made up of approximately 3.2 billion base pairs of DNA. The average human chromosome about 5 centimeters of DNA and considering all 23 pairs of chromosomes, there are approximately 2 meters of DNA packed into the nucleus of each of our cells.[74]

The developments leading to such information, were part of the post-World War II explosion in genomic research which culminated in the Human Genome project. This project was a massive ($3.0 Billion) government funded international effort to sequence, or map out, all the genes comprising the human genome. Planning began in 1984 and the project was completed in 2003, (two years ahead of schedule). The project and its successful outcome, inspired an even greater increase in genetic research throughout the world resulting in countless medical breakthroughs, and holding out the not unreasonable expectations for vastly improved human life in the future.

Among the many important findings of the current research is a more complete understanding of the role and process of mutations in natural selection. Mutations are very common, but the only ones that count (for evolutionary purposes), are mutations in the germ cells (the reproductive cells), because these are the only ones that are heritable.

---

[73] It has been estimated that there about 37 trillion cells in the human body. However, authorities are divided as to how many of these 37 trillion cells are red blood cells having no nucleus and thus carrying no DNA. Estimates seem to vary between 80% to 50%., which would suggest that there could be 8-18 trillion somatic cells in the human body. I will assume the higher number.

[74] John Archibold. *Genomics,* (Oxford: Oxford University Press, 2018) 8.

The human genome project enabled researchers to determine that a typical individual will carry about 63 new mutations upon birth.[75] Some of these mutations may be favorable inasmuch as they produce a small genetic advantage, some may be benign, and some may be unfavorable. The whole concept of evolution is founded on the notion that the accretion of many very small advantageous mutations will allow the "improved" organism to prevail, and ultimately emerge as the sole representative of the species. In fact, it explains the advance of the whole 3.5 billion year evolution of animate life from the simplicity of the single cell eukaryotes up through the extraordinary complexity of the human animal.

But, science is relentless in its advance. Lately (during the past decade), research is providing evidence that seems to support the idea of epigenetic influences on species development, holding out the possibility that certain acquired traits may be subject to inheritance. (A Lamarckian heresy in the world of Darwinian science.) Also, Darwin's foundational theory of the accretion of many very small mutations gradually causing change, has been successfully challenged by the results of recent research indicating that large mutational jumps can occur, and do in fact, occur routinely.

All this science-this genomic science-is very new indeed. And this is the point of the last few paragraphs. After all, it was only sixteen years ago that the human genome was first sequenced. So, it is not surprising that theologians and philosophers have yet to catch up.

DNA and Abortion: Some Simple Lessons

Keeping in mind that while this entire essay is about good and evil, this particular section is pointed at the morality of abortion, which I consider to be the "Big Evil" of our times. Unlike many such discussions, I will undertake this analysis solely from a cellular perspective. Too often, people are dismissive of the cell, even the embryonic stem cell. I believe to the contrary that the most important discussions regarding

---

[75] Jonathon Slack. *Genes*, (Oxford: Oxford University Press, 2014) 39.

the morality of abortion should begin at the cellular level. And, of course, what is true of the cell, is in a different way, equally true of the fetus. So, here we go.

All my life, I have heard the mantra: "Life begins at conception". Among Catholics that means that ensoulment begins at conception. And all my life, I have responded with the skeptical statement: "How do you know that!", "Prove it". And, all my life, my suspicions were confirmed. They never could prove it.

When pressed, theologians would admit as much, but would quickly respond by pointing out that the matter) is of such gravity that one has no choice but to assume that life begins at conception, for to do otherwise risks unthinkable moral error. I have found that to be a compelling argument.

Now, as it turns out, advances in genomic science with respect to the DNA molecule and its interaction with other elements of the human cell, may ultimately lead to a broad consensus among members of the scientific community that the probability of human life beginning at conception is not an unrealistic expectation. Old prejudices and old ideas die hard, but the weight of accumulated evidence may become overwhelming. That said, there is nothing now, nor is it likely there ever will be anything in the future, that will identify when the spirit (soul) joins with the human being, which from a theological perspective, constitutes the definition of the human person.

On the other hand, if the human (without regard to soul or spirit) can be thought as an organism with an intellectual capacity, traditionally defined as a "rational animal", then I think it is possible to say that, in principal, 'life' does begin at conception. Here are the facts to date.

What we have learned is that the DNA molecule, (the one used to trace your ancestry, or solve crimes), contains an incomprehensibly vast amount of information far in excess of that which we commonly hear about. An organism's DNA is a finely detailed template of its hosts existence. Absent a person's DNA, there is no person. The DNA molecule is a complete description and governor of all of a person's genetic make-up. And while life experience may provide enrichment that could modify one's behavior, it can do so only within the constraints of the underlying genetic predisposition found in its DNA. However, more often than not, the way people think, the way they behave, their intellectual capacity, their physical abilities, their emotional strengths and weaknesses, how, when and who they love, their resistance to disease, their predisposition to life shortening infirmities, their rate of growth and maturation, and even their probable life span, are to be found only in the person's unique DNA molecule. This wonderous object, the DNA molecule, is present in at least half of our 37 trillion cells, (the remaining half are red blood cells which have no nucleus). DNA is not just an enabler of human life, it is life itself. Take away one's DNA and there is no life as a human person.[76]

DNA is located within the cell. It cannot exist, nor can it do its work, without the supporting framework of the cell in which it resides. DNA itself, is not a living organism. It needs the cellular mechanism to function and to become a part of life.

The DNA molecule is found primarily within the cell's nucleus, with a small part also found within the mitochondria. The composition of the cell is not simple. In addition to the nucleus and its incorporated DNA, the principal components are: the shell or the Plasma Membrane, the Nucleolus, the Endoplasmic Reticulum, the Golgi apparatus, the Mitochondria, Lysosomes, Peroxisomes, Microtubules and Microfilaments, and the Cytosol.

The Nucleus synthesizes (manufactures) DNA and RNA, the Nucleolus synthesizes Ribosomes, the Endoplasmic Reticulum synthesizes proteins, steroids and lipids. The Golgi apparatus processes and exports proteins, the Mitochondria produces ATP which is the energy for the cell, it also aids in cellular respiration, Lysosomes signal Apoptosis (cellular death) and conduct cellular digestion, Peroxisomes aid in lipid oxidation, Microtubules and Microfilaments are the

---

[76] As Christians we believe that humans are composed of body and soul. The body is the material part and the soul is the immaterial or spiritual part. So, how does the soul communicate, interact, or influence it material counterpart? Aquinas says the body and soul are united as a single entity with the soul being the form of the body, even though the soul can continue to live after the death of the body. But what, exactly. Is the point of contact?

'skeleton' of the cell and provide for intracellular movement, the Cytosol metabolizes carbohydrates.

Cells are the building blocks of the body. Apart from Germ cells they are differentiated by the special functions they perform. For instance, there are nerve cells, muscle cells, skin cells, etc. However, every cell, except the red blood cell, has in common, a set of basic functions. In general, the functions, common to all but red blood cells, are as follows: (1) to cause the host organisms to develop, grow, and repair itself by self-replication through cell division (mitosis in all but germ cells); and (2) to cause the host organism to grow, develop, and repair itself by producing and exporting the necessary new proteins and lipids as specified by the cell's DNA.

The process of cell division begins with the cell producing an exact copy of each of its many components. Once this is completed and once there is sufficient energy and nutrients to assure continued life for the parent cell and it's daughter cell, the activity of division then creates two identical cells where once there was one. In a mature human, about three billion cells die and are replaced every day. As for protein and lipid production, the process to synthesize and transport proteins and lipids starts with the DNA which codes for a specific protein intended for an identifiable location. The code is transcribed to a messenger RNA molecule, which then moves outside the nucleus to the endoplasmic reticulum where it is processed and then transferred to a ribosome where the code is translated to produce the protein. The ribosome then moves to the Golgi apparatus where the protein is encased in a vesicle for movement through the cell membrane to its intended destination.[77]

The last few paragraphs, while not having much to do with theology, are intended to provide an abbreviated overview of some of the operations and functions of the human cell to provide context to what follows. Biologists would find this summary grossly incomplete (and I would agree). However, the purpose is not so much to teach a

---

[77] Much of the information regarding the components of the cell and their functions has been drawn from: Thomas M. Devlin. "Eukaryotic Cell Structure" in *Textbook of Biochemistry With Clinical Correlations,* ed. Thomas M. Devlin, (New York: John Wiley & Sons, Inc. 2011), 1-21.

lesson in science as it is to illustrate the extraordinary complexity of the cell, and, in fact, the extraordinary complexity of life itself.; always keeping in mind that this hive of cellular activity is fast, continuous and with multiple functionality that occurs simultaneously in many regions throughout the cell – an object so unimaginably minute that there are about 1.5 billion cells comprising a single index finger.[78]

Now to the creation of new human life. The first glimmer of human life is the fertilized human egg, called the *zygote*. It is a single cell and it contains the DNA molecule that is unique only to itself. That this single cell is a new and separate unit of life should be evident to all, because it has its own DNA, and also because it fulfills the fundamental definition of life as described by molecular biologists, Terrence Allen and Graham Cowling.:

> The cell is the basic unit of life, and as such must fulfill three requirements: (1) to be a separate entity, requiring a surface membrane; (2) to interact with the surrounding environment to extract energy in some way for maintenance and growth; (3) to replicate itself. These parameters are the same for all living beings, from the smallest bacterium, to any one of the 200 different cell types that create the human being.[79]

Add to this, the human DNA, and you have a potential human person all wrapped up in a single cell. But this thing, the *zygote*, is not just a simple little insignificant entity, as the proponents of abortion would have you believe, it is an extraordinarily complex organism.

First of all, the *zygote* is a unique type of cell created only upon fertilization of the egg by the sperm. It is a stem cell. Most importantly,

---

[78] If there are 37 trillion cells comprising the human body, and the mass of the index finger is approximately 1/4000 of the mass of the entire body, then there are 1.5 billion cells of all kinds (skin, bone, blood, muscle, fat, nerve, and endothelial) comprising an index finger..

[79] Terence Allen and Graham Cowling, *The Cell*. (Oxford: Oxford University Press, 2011) 3.

it is a 'totipotent' stem cell, that is to say, unlike ordinary somatic cells which produce additional cells that are only of the same specialization as itself (e.g. muscle cells, skin cells, etc.), the totipotent cell is one that can divide and produce all the differentiated cells of the organism. Immediately after fertilization, the *zygote* produces identical totipotent cells which after approximately four days begin to specialize into the differentiated requirements of the now growing human being.

Individual differentiated cells carry out the process of growth which will continue without interruption throughout the entire life of the human. They do so by mitosis or cell division and by the production of new proteins and lipids. Here are Alan and Cowing on the subject of cell division:

> The actual mechanics of cell division,... require significantly more instructions than it takes to build a moon rocket or supercomputer. First of all, the cell needs to duplicate all of its molecules, that is DNA, RNA, proteins, lipids, etc. At the organelle level, several hundred mitochondria, large areas of ER, new Golgi bodies, cytoskeletal structures, and ribosomes by the millions all need to be duplicated so the daughter cells have enough resources to grow and in turn divide themselves.[80]

This is the operation of a typical somatic cell, but when we move up to the operation of the totipotent *zygote* we enter a new dimension of complexity, one which even now is but imperfectly understood by present day biologists, and one which is the focus of intense research.

In order to grasp the amazing-almost miraculous- capability of the *zygote* to produce all the different types of the human cell, the following paragraph is a summary list of these types. (This is tedious reading. It is provided only to illustrate the breadth and depth of the *zygote's* capability.)

---

[80] Ibid., 60.

Nine exocrine secretory epithelial cells, such as the gland in the duodenum that secretes enzymes and alkaline mucus. Five <u>barrier cells</u> such as the gall bladder epithelial cell. Twenty <u>hormone secreting cells</u>, such as the G cell that secretes gastrin, or the pancreatic beta cell that secretes insulin and amylin. Twelve <u>exocrine secretory epithelial cells</u>, such as the salivary gland or the mammary gland. Ten <u>hormone secreting cells</u>, such as chromaffin cells which comprise the adrenal gland. Fifteen <u>epithelial cells</u>, such as the trichocyte that gives rise to hair and nail cells. Eighteen <u>sensory transducer cells</u>, such as heat sensitive primary sensory neurons or the photoreceptor cells of the retina. Three <u>autonomic neuron cells</u>. Twelve <u>sense organ and peripheral neuron supporting cells</u>, such as the olfactory epithelium supporting cell. Thirty different <u>central nervous system and glial cells</u>. Two <u>lens cells</u>. Three <u>metabolism and storage cells</u>, such as white and brown fat cells. Eighteen <u>secretory cells</u>, such as the prostrate gland of the uterus endometrium cell that secretes carbohydrates. Eight <u>urinary barrier cells</u>. Four types of <u>reproductive barrier cells</u>. One type of <u>endothelial circulatory cell</u>. Seventeen <u>extracellular matrix cells</u>, such as found in tendons, bone marrow and cartilage. Twelve types of <u>contractile cells</u>, such as are found in skeletal or cardiac muscles. Twenty one <u>blood and immune system cells</u> such as red and white blood cells. Five <u>germ cells</u>. Three <u>nurse cells</u>.[81]

There are 229 different types of cells listed above, all with highly differentiated characteristics, and all derived from the single totipotent stem cell, the *Zygote*. Every single type of cell in the body is listed here. Each will continue throughout the life of the organism to elaborate its part of the creative growth process through mitosis and the production of cell specific proteins. But, only the *zygote* functions without limits, for it will originate all of the different types of cells. In fact, it is their sole source. Thus, the *zygote,* through its unique DNA and its extraordinary cellular function, could be thought of as the entire human being capsulized in a single cell.

---

[81] https://en.wikipedia.org/wik/list_of_distinct_cell_types_in_the_human_body. Page last edited on 21 August, 2019. Accessed on 22August, 2019.

Does this sound like something that is "just a meaningless bundle of nothing" which is the prevailing theme of those who promote the hyper-selfishness of abortion? Of course not!

What it clearly shows is the absurdity of the abortionists logic, for even at its origin, its most primary cellular level, the fetus is a unique human.

Each embryonic stem cell, each *zygote*, occurs only once in history. This individual cell never occurred in the past, there are no others like it in the present, and it will never again exist in the future. It is singular and unique. In its DNA and in its cellular structure, it incorporates all that is necessary to develop into a unique human being. Absent external force or external circumstances, it is nearly 100% certain that given nutrition and time, it will become an independent person.

Yet, curiously much of the public seems to accept the oft-repeated political argument in justification of abortion that asserts: "A women's body is hers and she can do with it anything she desires.

This argument, of course, displays almost laughable ignorance. It is hard to imagine a more misinformed position, because the indisputable scientific answer is that: "The zygote is not her body! It's not even a part of her body, never was, nor ever will be. It is a separate and unique organism". There is no ambiguity here. Yet, this is not the infant-like image the pro-life people often show to appeal to one's emotions. Not hardly--this is a near invisible single cell. A picture shows nothing that resembles a human. Nevertheless, as demonstrated by the evidence provided by advanced cellular biology, this single cell really is a human.

Among the world-wide scientific community, especially those engaged in biological research, these is nearly universal agreement that human life begins at conception. Francis Collins, one the world's most distinguished genetic biologists affirms this truth by specifying that:

> "from a biologist's perspective, the steps that follow the union of sperm and egg occur in a highly predictable order, leading to increased complexity, and with no sharp boundaries between phases. There is no

convenient biological dividing line between a human being and an embryonic form…"[82]

So, I leave it to the reader. ….Is to kill a *zygote* to kill a human being? Science seems to think it is[83]. And so do I, because given the weight of evidence, I do not see how one could come to any other conclusion.

But, to the zealots, those who are inspired and energized by their own peculiar ideology, it doesn't make any difference. Whether the *zygote* (or fetus) is human or not, is simply not relevant. Other factors, mainly personal, social, emotional, and even political, outweigh the facts of biology. In that light, recalling the earlier discussion of the connection between "Big Evil", ideology, and the suspension of reason, I do not think it unreasonable to assert that: if ever there were the quintessential example of ideology configuring and inspiring evil, the abortion movement is it.' (Please see also p.73-76).

****

---

[82] Collins 2006, 250.

[83] While the scientific facts objectively stated, affirm the humanity of the *zygote*, many and perhaps most scientists, will have difficulty in reaching full agreement with that statement. Scientists, after all, are members of a community and as such, are no less immune from the opinions and biases of their community than anyone else. When it comes to the matter of abortion, the personal, emotional and political sense of society will inevitably influence the judgements of most of its members. Scientists are no exception. Notwithstanding clear evidence, it certainly took a long time for the scientific community to find truth in the dangers of global climate change. Such also was the case in the 1940's and 1950's with the health risk posed by smoking. And in an interesting episode from history when the Copernican heliocentric theory was first published in 1543, the stars were embedded in a solid sphere surrounding the rest of the universe. This allowed Copernicus to satisfy the bias of Catholic culture and society which needed a distant and inaccessible place for God and the Angels. It wasn't until 1576, that Thomas Digges, an English mathematician, not under the influence of the Catholic church, completed the Copernican theory by scattering the stars randomly through an infinite space, with no hard shell surrounding the universe. So, even with Copernicus, objectivity was impaired.

Much of this advanced biological science that has been the focus of the preceding pages, has emerged only within recent decades, and it will likely take a long time for it to fully penetrate the public consciousness. The ideology promoting and enabling mass abortion is so deeply embedded in our culture that even when the cellular and genomic sciences become widely known, many generations will have passed before the ideologues of mass abortion will finally yield to the truths of science. But, just as occurred during the Enlightenment, it is certain that science and truth will ultimately prevail over ignorance and ideology.

VII

Final Thoughts

The Question of Metaphysics

In various places within this paper, I have been dismissive of Aristotelian metaphysics as expressed in the works of St. Thomas Aquinas and the Scholastics. My dissatisfaction has two sources. The first relates to the attempts, by the scholars of antiquity, to understand nature in grand theories with little recourse to hard empirical data, and without verification by observation of the real world. And this itself is rooted in two limitations that constrained their efforts, the first being the lack of instrumentation, and the second being lack of capacity to communicate with other scholars or researchers. Here I am referring to the momentous impact of the printing press, and then the revolution in electronic communications right up to the present day when researchers can share information globally in real time. This is of vital importance because science, and knowledge in general, builds upon itself in thousands of minute incremental steps; and the ancient's lacking this critical advantage, (as well as their inability to systematically test their theories), forced them to create imaginary castles in the air. The second source of my dissatisfaction with Aristotelian metaphysics has to do with its underlying assumption. It is grounded on the assumption of an unchanging, static universe fully complete upon its creation. Yet we now know that this is simply not true. It is now acknowledged by everyone, except religious fundamentalists, that the evolutionary principle is the foundation upon which the universe was conceived. From the Big Bang, which started with a fog of disorganized sub-atomic particles to the present, 13.7 billion years later, the universe has been a place of unending change as the simplest particles, quickened by the four fundamental forces and their own internal dynamics, combine and recombine themselves in an interminable drive towards ever increasing complexity, culminating in the emergence of life, which in turn, increases complexity by perhaps an order of magnitude, or even greater.

Ilia Delio, OSF, a prominent scholar of Teilhardian thought frames this subject in the following manner:

> Metaphysics is the study of principles underlying reality: the nature and purpose of being. Christianity inherited a metaphysics based on Greek philosophy, formed against a stable, fixed cosmos. Scholastic theologians constructed teachings on creation, salvation, and redemption based on the principles of Greek metaphysics.
>
> Teilhard's "hyperphysics" is a foundational first step towards renewing Christianity in an evolutionary universe, moving beyond a static metaphysics of being.
>
> Instead of a metaphysics of being which connotes stability and sameness, he suggested that a metaphysics of unity had emerged: 'Let us replace a metaphysics of *Esse* by a metaphysics of *Unire*.' The foundation of existence is not mere being itself (what is) but relationality (what is becoming): union is always towards more being.
>
> Teilhard coined the word "hyperphysics" to describe a principle of more being; that is, the fundamental drive of everything is towards *more being*." [84]

---

[84] Ilia Delio, OSF, "Evolution and the Rise of the Secular God" in *From Teilhard to Omega*, ed. Ilia Delio, (Maryknoll, New York: Orbis Books, 2014) 42.

That said, I would offer the thought that in the Thomistic assertion that being is sustained only by the will and active participation of God at all times, there may be an avenue in traditional Catholicism for its enrichment by incorporating the Teilhardian evolutionary insights.

Words and Concepts Appropriate to Their Times

A common theme throughout this paper is that, many interpretations of biblical truths as promoted within the Catholic church are, not only erroneous, but also, (in light of contemporary science), so improvidently misleading that they spawn apostasy. Young people with little more than a high school education can easily see the stark disagreement between elementary science, and Church teachings, most of which have not been updated for as much as two thousand years. The world has changed. It is no longer a place where heat and light come from the hearth, medicine from blood-letters, transportation by donkeys, and communication by word of mouth or hand inscribed parchments. Yet, our Church insists on formulating essential truths in language and with concepts, that are centuries beyond being obsolete.

In the preceding pages, I have addressed, in a very perfunctory manner, certain questions surrounding the formulation of the doctrine of the Trinity, the means by which we explain the existence of a creator God, the matter of original sin, the fable of "The Fall of Man," and the nature of evil. All of these, and many other teachings, must be reconfigured and adapted to current realities. Otherwise, the Church will continue to become increasingly irrelevant in the lives of a greater and greater numbers of people. The job is not difficult, but overcoming the inevitable resistance is.

I will leave the last words on this subject to Joseph Ratzinger, Pope Benedict XVI, which he preached in the Lenten homilies at the cathedral church of Munich in the late winter of 1981. Describing how one should read and understand the creation story in Genesis; he says:

One must distinguish between the form of the portrayal and the content that is portrayed. The form would have been chosen from that what was understandable at the time—from images which surrounded the people who lived then, which they used in speaking and thinking, and thanks to which they were able to understand the greater realities. And only the reality that shines through these images would be what was intended and what was truly enduring.[85]

Ideology as the Means by Which Satan Accomplishes His Objectives in the World.

Earlier in this paper, I offered the opinion that ideologies are the means by which Satan attempts to impose his will on the universe. This proposal is made within the wider context of two types of evil: natural and moral. Natural evils are things like sickness, disease, natural disasters, and death. Moral evils are the bad things one person does to another; the suffering inflicted by man upon creation. Moral evil is mainly the consequence of man's genetically imposed inclination towards selfishness as expressed by the drive for self-preservation and reproduction. In this interpretation, almost all moral evil can be explained by the natural extension and distortion of the evolutionary principal. However, some eruptions of moral evil, like the Holocaust, are of such a scale and so heinous as to defy any explanation other than the influence of "the evil one"; Satan, operating through corrupt ideologies.

So, what do I mean when I use the term ideology? How is it defined?

My understanding is that an ideology is a body of beliefs that guides individuals, social and political movements, class and large groups, marked by the following attributes:

---

[85] Joseph Ratzinger, *In the Beginning...A Catholic Understanding of the Story of Creation and the Fall,* translated by Boniface Ramsey, O.P. (Grand Rapids, Michigan: William Eerdmans Publishing Company, 1995), 5.

- It is a system of thought that interprets and explains the world
- It is normative as to beliefs, values, and action.
- It implies a strict moral code in which all behavior is subject only to its own norms.
- It is exclusive and all-encompassing. It alone projects the truth. All other systems of thought are invalid, and must be repressed, (even to the point of violence).
- Religions can be an ideology
- Above all: **Unreserved adherence to an ideology always implies the suspension of reason.**

In most cases, ideological or Satanic motivation will be found mixed with biological or Darwinian motivation. Here are some examples from recent history:

The First World War. The war itself was one originated in the milieu of economic nationalism and the balance of powers. It was clearly a war of self-interest. But it was in the execution of the war that ideology came into play. This was the ideology of class superiority which provided a moral justification for the massacre of millions. And it was the Class System that provided the normative body of beliefs that guided the actions of the leaders on both sides. The war effectively put an end to the ideology of class. A total of 16.0 million people died.

Ukrainian and Kazakh Genocide.

The ideology of Communism, adopted by Russia in 1917, mandated the abandonment of private property. In agricultural region's this was accomplished by forceful collectivization. In order to implement the collectivization of agriculture, and also to repress other values (such as Christianity), the Russian government, in the period 1932-33, initiated a genocide by enforced famine. Approximately 7.0 million Ukrainians and Kazakhs died in this unambiguous eruption of pure ideological evil.

World War Two.

This conflict, initiated by Germany and Japan, was clearly a war of national expansion. However, in the case of both countries the aggression was masked by a deeply embedded ideology of racism. German culture, especially in the inter-war period was overwhelmed by the concept of Aryan racial superiority. In Japan, the historical word commonly used to describe people from another country is *gaijin*, which in English translates to" barbarian", and, in fact, reflects the attitude of the Japanese people as regards all non-Japanese. This cultural prevarication prevails even today among all but the most cosmopolitan class. The ideology of racial superiority infected the entirety of both Germany and Japan, and provided the moral foundation for enslaving the "sub-human" Slavic peoples and "barbaric" Koreans. Approximately 60 million people died in this war of expansion that successfully established its legitimacy among its own people by means of an ideology of racial superiority.

<u>The Jewish Holocaust During World War II.</u>

The whole story is too well known to repeat here. However, what is unbelievable, except for the fact that it really happened, was that the thousands (maybe hundreds of thousands) of individuals who carried out the industrialized slaughter of the "Final Solution," believed that their actions were good and were moral. This mass suspension of accepted morality, demonstrating the effect of ideology is, far and away, the most frightening aspect of this horror, because it absolutely defies reason, and has never been explained.

<u>Mao's Great Leap Forward.</u>

This was China's successful implementation of the agricultural collectivization mandated by adherence to the ideology of Communism. It was accomplished by means of a forced famine in which an estimated 30 million people died in the period 1958-62. Again, as with the Holocaust and the Ukrainian famine, hundreds of thousands of police and government functionaries believing in the morality of an ideology, directly caused the deaths of those with whom they came in daily contact without a tremor of conscience believing that their actions were moral and good because their actions were validated by the ideology.

<u>Worldwide Fetal Extinction by Abortion.</u>

In the United States, since Roe v. Wade, there have been 61 million abortions; 18 million, or 30% were African-American, (a demographic group that represents 13% of the total population). According to the Guttmacher Institute, in 2003, there were about 1.5 million abortions in North America. Worldwide, there were 42 million abortions: 26 million in Asia, 4 million in Europe, 6 million in Africa, and 4 million in Latin America.[86] Notice that nearly 10 million abortions were in nominally Christian regions where one might have expected the Gospel message to have penetrated.

Will this nightmare ever end? I don't know about other parts of the world, but as for the United States, I believe there are realistic grounds for hope.

Future generations of Americans, I believe, will look back with shame and horror at the mass abortion slaughter of the 20th-21st century. They will see it in much the same way as we today, see the nightmare of the Holocaust and the evils of slavery. They will wonder how people could morally justify such actions as extinguishing human life for nothing more substantive than personal convenience. They will be puzzled how supposedly civilized people could have lived with such things.

Sometime in the near future, probably in our great-grandchildren's lifetime, there will be a sudden turn in public attitudes regarding abortion. The momentum of bio-genetic research makes this a certainty, for the arc of scientific development is like an arrow pointing relentlessly in a single direction. And that direction is one which will establish in the minds of the public, what science already suspects, that the human embryo, even the *zygote*, is a complete human being upon conception. There will be no room for doubt.

The science will likely be completed within our grandchildren's lifetime. In addition to this proof of life, we can expect to see genetic engineering solutions to the embryonic developmental problems currently leading to unfavorable birth outcomes. Abnormalities like Down's syndrome, mental retardation, and other complex learning issues, physical deformities, and the propensity for life shortening illness, that had previously justified abortion, will be a thing of the past.

---

[86] Sasheela Singh et. al. *Abortion Worldwide: A Decade of Uneven Progress*, (New York: Guttmacher Institute, 2009) 51.

On first impression, such a prediction may seem far-fetched. But here is Developmental Biologist, Scott Gilbert, Distinguished Finland Professor at the University of Helsinki, and senior research fellow at Swarthmore College who provides the following observation regarding the development of the human brain:

> Both humans and other apes have rapid brain growth before birth. However, whereas the brain growth slows considerably in other apes, the growth of the human brain continues at the fetal rate for around two years, making over thirty thousand new synapses per second.
> Some of the genes that differ between humans and other apes are those genes that accelerate human brain growth.[87]

To put this into perspective, synapses are what connect the neurons (nerve cells) to one another. Neurons process and communicate information. There are about 86 billion neurons in a typical human brain. Each neuron is connected to as many as 10,000 other neurons by a network comprising more than 100 trillion synapses. Now, if Gilbert is correct and developing humans can produce thirty thousand new connections (synapses) per second for two years after birth, whereas apes cannot, then one might reasonably hypothesize that the same variation in rate of synapse production that differentiates man from ape, might also play a role in the mental development of retarded, autistic or other mentally challenged humans. Said differently, if such people are fruit of an abnormal rate of synapse production, then a solution may be possible by finding the genetic factors that cause such a rate.

Enter now, researchers from the Baylor University Medical School in Houston, who, in 2007, determined that the protein MeCP2 is essential to the fine tuning of synapse production. In addition, they found

---

[87] Scott F. Gilbert. "Evolution Through Developmental Change." *In Darwin in the Twenty First Century*, edited by Phillip Sloan, Gerald McKenny, Kathleen Eggleson. (Notre Dame: University of Notre Dame Press, 2015).

that an imbalance, that is to say, too much or too little MeCP2, can directly result in mental retardation, autism and other related functional failures. This protein is produced in a human's cells. It is a product of genetic activity regulated by the individual's DNA, and this holds out the possibility that it may be manipulated by human intervention.

However, this is a layman's hypothesis, and thus, it is pure conjecture whether such an advance is possible, and even if possible, it would be many years before medical science or bioengineering could use such information to prevent mental handicaps as were found correlated with the cellular production of proteins like MeCP2.[88]

Nevertheless, in the future, bio-engineering may give us perfect outcomes for every birth. However, while this is going on, the reactionary and conservative religious elements in society (including the Catholic church) will likely resist such developments because they will be seen a interfering with the "natural order."[89] Meanwhile, the progressive, highly-educated elites who today constitute the core support for mass abortion, will strongly encourage such scientific initiatives, not

---

[88] Baylor College of Medicine. "Brain Needs Perfection in Synapse Number." *ScienceDaily*. ScienceDaily, 8 October 2007. (www. Sciencedaily.com/releases/2007/10/071003130855.htm)

[89] Bio-engineering as used in this paper is otherwise known as Eugenics. The ethical and moral issues surrounding the practice of eugenics are manifold. We have seen terrible examples of this practice in the 20th century. Yet, notwithstanding such atrocities as the Nazi's WWII program of racial purity through eugenics, it is my prediction that society will come to terms with its misgivings (perhaps through law and regulation) and in the interest of clear medical benefits will endorse a positive form of eugenics at molecular level. This will create a crisis for the Catholic Church, as the Church will be then confronted by an unambiguous dilemma. On the one hand there will be the paired combination of birth control and bio-engineering which will serve to justify the abandonment of abortion as an accepted practice; on the other hand there is the reality of mass abortion which will continue if alternatives are withheld or not available. It's a simple binary decision. However, in this matter, as well as other similar matters such as invitro fertilization, the Church will need to decide whether or not to value life as mandated by Scripture, or continue in its blind adherence to man-made philosophical constructs, which have the effect of facilitating the destruction of life.

really comprehending the connection to their favorite cause. But their grandchildren will. It is they who will lead the transformation of public attitudes, much like their grandparents led the transformation in public attitudes towards gays, lesbians, and transsexuals.

All this may be the future. If history is any guide it will surely occur. I cannot see how it could be otherwise. However, as for today, right now in our own society, among our own neighbors, and every day before our eyes, the ideologically inspired evil of mass abortion is occurring as a matter of routine acceptable behavior. Any threat or limitation to this practice is met with violent, irrational, panic stricken response. There is no room for discussion or reason. The venomous hostility is instantaneous.

I see its empowering ideology as one rooted in a sort of hyper-selfishness, which I would define as an irrational extension of the genetically imposed characteristic of human and animal selfishness as discussed earlier in this paper. Such selfishness in its natural or ordinary form, despite its many problems, is a positive good, insofar as it is the heart of the evolutionary principal enabling all human development. Thus, in the context and language of this paper, Darwinian selfishness (a good) is corrupted to become a source of unequivocal evil. How does this happen?

It happens because ideologies that command such disordered loyalty, cannot possibly have a human origin, not at least if we believe humans to be rational. Thus, I hold that these types of ideologies can be explained only by the intervention of an influence outside of the human orbit. Moral evil in the form of selfishness, which can be an evil within the human orbit, explains all examples of harm committed by individuals and most harm committed by nations or groups of people. However, when it comes to moral evil on a massive scale, evil that requires <u>the suspension of reason</u>, not for just for a few people, but for a mass population who uniformly accepts an ideological morality at variance with both reason and custom, there is no explanation other than the intervention of the supernatural principal of evil that scripture calls Satan, or The Evil One. [90]

The suffering, the harm, and the deaths associated with the 20th century examples of Big Evil all have one thing in common. And that is a specific ideology for each event that in establishing its own morality, requires the mass suspension of the rational principal – a principal that defines humanity. The obscenity of the Holocaust has frequently been described as a descent into bestiality; and in my judgement, that is exactly what it is. The obscenity of mass abortion is the same. History conclusively demonstrates that the adherents of such ideologies, as those described above, become less than fully human as they become more subservient to Satanic influence. And while there is hope for those in demographic groups that will finally comprehend the errors of their ideology, one must ask, what about the rest? [91]

Is There a Teleological Direction to the Universe?

The definition of "teleological" is as follows: Teleological refers to the explanation of phenomena in terms of the purpose they serve (or final cause) rather than the cause by which they arise. It is commonly associated with explanations of nature by reference to design, or more specifically, design provided by a divine cause (God).

Almost all scholars, scientists and historians, reject the idea of a teleological cause. While, they may identify, and build into their scholarly work, the notion of direction in the universe, reliance on God as a cause of anything is a scientific anathema. The perceived direction over deep time is from simplicity to complexity. Thus there is common

---

[90] In today's world, it is not common among progressive theologians to refer to Satan as an operative principal or cause of moral action. In fact, most prefer to ignore the whole idea of Satan. Yet, in the context of Christian theology, Satan cannot be ignored. By my count, he is testified a total of thirty-five separate times in the New Testament. And, in a work such as this, Scripture is fundamental.

[91] Here, I am referring mainly to the millions in Africa, Asia, and Latin America. If their government's fail to provide and encourage easy access to free birth control, the slaughter will continue.

agreement that a sort of evolutionary principal is at work in both the physical and biological worlds.

Moreover, it is not unusual to find this direction expressed as phases: a geo-phase (geosphere) and a bio-phase (geosphere). In the geosphere, from the disorganized mass of sub-atomic particles at the instant of the singularity known as the Big Bang, to the complex physical structures comprising the universe as we now know it, there has been an uninterrupted thrust from simplicity to complexity. Likewise, in biosphere, from the simplicity of the first living things, through the single celled organisms (prokaryotes), to the complexity of large mammals, and finally to the additional complexity of the human mind, there also has been a consistent evolutionary train from simplicity to complexity.

Scientists reject the very idea of an outside cause, asserting instead, that the movement from simplicity to complexity is the result of internal forces and the dynamics of their interactions over time. Here is a description of one way this might have occurred:

> One answer to the origin of complexity is surprisingly simple. There are forces between objects. Some forces-like gravity and the opposite poles of magnets-repel. If we could turn the clock back and distribute the matter of the universe evenly, the particles would immediately start their dance of attraction and repulsion....as they attract each other they would congregate to form clumps. Once that happens we break the symmetry of a perfectly uniform universe. Those clumps would form initially as clouds and then as stars and planets.[92]

This is not dispositive, but it certainly does illustrate the kind of reasoning that, if adequately supported with physical evidence of broad application, might be more universal and thus more compelling.

---

[92] Noble.,124.

However, this is a work of theology, and for us, the notion of God as the Final Cause of creation is not merely a nice idea, it is the foundation of our thinking. Theilhard constructed his entire theological framework on the twin pillars of God as the final of cause, and the evolutionary principal as the means by which life finds union with God.

Theilhard understood evolution to move through its biological phase to a concluding phase in which humankind progresses into the Noosphere, that is to say, to the world of the mind which becomes progressively spiritual culminating with union with Christ (God). Often his theories are summarized as directed movement from simplicity, through increasing complexity, to consciousness. Sixty years ago, when first exposed to these ideas, I could not understand how such an apparent fantasy could come about. I still can't. But, I think it may be possible to perceive the vague and cloudy outlines of Theilhard's directional thesis in the development of human knowledge.

This is not very difficult. If we survey the state of learning at the time of the ancient Greeks, say for example, 300 BCE, we know that their mastery of literature, philosophy, logic, and geometry was quite advanced. There is little that later generations have contributed. On the other hand, their knowledge of the sciences-physics, astronomy, chemistry, biology, genetics, calculus and other higher forms of mathematics, optics, geology, anthropology, etc. was all but non-existent. They were hopelessly ignorant. Moreover, lacking any means of mass communication, what little learning that the ancient's possessed was confined to a relatively small group of people, generally clustered around the Mediterranean basin.

I do not think it necessary to review the state of knowledge as it is today, however it definitely would be helpful to remind ourselves of the rate of increase in knowledge, and its fluidity, throughout the world. First, the printing press, and now the internet and various other forms of electronic communications, have permitted millions of minds to be engaged in the whole intellectual project. I sense that in recent decades, the rate of growth and spread of knowledge has accelerated from an arithmetic phase into a geometric phase. Where this is going and whether it is following a Theilhardian trajectory is pure speculation.

But, I have little doubt, that humanity is on the edge of an abyss leading to uncharted territory. Whether it will be good or evil is up to us.

Conclusion: Things to Ponder.

My objective in this theological study, has been to develop an analytical pathway to the problem of Theodicy through the use of a contemporary scientific framework. Of necessity, this approach is dismissive of the ancient Greek philosophical/scientific concepts traditionally used to interpret revelation.. Therefore, despite the my intermittint reliance on such insightful poetic and spiritual figures such as Dante, Milton, Von Speyer and Ekhart, mine is really a reductionist perspective. It is grounded on the evolutionary notion of all animate and inanimate creation inevitably moving from simplicity to complexity, over the 13.7 billion years of the history of the universe and beyond, as was first proposed in the 1930's by Pierre Theilhard de Chardin S.J. However, it also incorporates many of the scientific advances that have occurred since the death of Theilhard in what I hope would be seen as a complementary manner building upon Theilhard's fundamental thesis.

Two years ago when I started this personal journey, I had no idea how, where, or if, I would be able to arrive at a satisfactory outcome. Surprisingly, I now see the open road to a very optimistic future. The Theilhardian thesis that projects union with Christ in an undefined distant future certainly provides the substance of hope, but, also in the more immediate future, I see reason for hope. Much, however, depends upon the attitude and ultimately reformation of orthodox Christian praxis. And this is the 'wild-card'.

The Catholic Church should open its doors to substantive, and therefore determinative, lay participation in its governance at the highest levels. Only in this way will it be able to liberate itself from the constraints of obsolete interpretations that now present barriers to the theological opportunities that would flow from open research into the nexus of theology and science. Such research would not be to set up new dogmatic theses, (we've made that mistake in the past), but rather help the Church shed its overreliance on 'natural law' and ancient 'science', and thus, encourage a theological environment sufficiently open to freedom of thought so that it can acknowledge the ontological impenetrability of the Creator God, and rely once again on the inerrancy of revelation, except now in a new context, inspired by the advances in scientific knowledge.

Moreover, as noted above, this attempt to address the question of theodicy by reducing the concept of good and evil into elements to which the findings of contemporary science may be applied would likely precipitate the elimination of the ancient science that unfortunately has been historically intertwined with revelation. For example, the Aristotelian-Ptolemaic cosmology used to interpret Genesis and so deeply embedded in traditional Church culture, makes no sense in light of the Big Bang, and the entire Standard Cosmological Model. Similarly, the failure to acknowledge the truths of evolution, grievously impedes any serious attempt to explain evil.

And then, there is the question of ensoulment. We, as believing Christians, hold that humans are a composite of body and soul (or said differently matter and the Holy Spirit). But others, who constitute the overwhelming majority in the world's population, believe that a human is only matter. There is no spiritual element. Thus, for most people, abortion, (what I consider to be the consummate evil of our times), is no evil at all, since killing a *Zygote* (or a fetus), is viewed as no different than killing any other mammal. Why? Because neither the *zygote* nor the fetus possess the essential quality that differentiates a human from other mammals, namely, a functioning intellect. And this makes all the difference; for it is commonly thought that what distinguishes a human from all the other 5,400 species of mammalian life is the human's intellect--its ability to think.

Yet it is perfectly clear that when an infant is born, and for a year or more after birth, the human child also is indistinguishable from other mammals, because it too, does not have a functioning intellect. It cannot think. However, what it unquestionably does have, is the potential to develop a functioning intellect as the brain synapses develop over the first two years of life. (see page 68).

But then, one must ask: how does this differ from the *Zygote*? Well the answer is obvious. In terms of potential, the two--the Zygote and infant child,--are identical. The *Zygote* has the potential to develop into a complete person, and in the normal course of time, will inevitably do so. In like manner, the newly born infant, who cannot even feed itself, will similarly develop into a complete person. Yet aborting the *Zygote* or the fetus, is thought to be morally acceptable, while infanticide is not.

This inconsistency certainly merits more thorough investigation as well as serious research, not only by the scientific community, but also, by the theological community. But, where, one must ask, is the Catholic church in all of this?

Well that's easy. It's stuck in the Middle Ages. Apart from ignoring the science, such as that discussed throughout this paper, the Vatican refuses to face the plain fact that to end the horror of mass fetal killings, it must offer a practical alternative, which implies that it must cooperate in the wide-spread distribution of effective birth control. Yet, on questionable scriptural grounds coupled with specious logic, the Church does just the opposite. And that is why I earlier suggested that the Catholics will be hard pressed to cure the moral evils of society, (some of which are of the Vatican's own making), without a substantial lay presence in the highest governing levels of the Church to lead it's clerical establishment out of their insular, self-referential paralysis, (or inability) to walk away from the outdated and fallacious teachings sadly issued by their predecessors.

There are many non-traditional idea's set forth in this monograph, but none so provocative as to suggest that the Catholic church should not only abandon its historic opposition to birth control but, more radically, should actively promote the use of such means to serve as an alternative to abortion. Yet, notwithstanding the merits of the argument, it is unlikely to ever be a serious topic of discussion within the halls of the Vatican, because its denizens, even when their intent is pure, consistently get themselves paralyzed over the question of precedent, prior practice, and their delusionary conceit that all teachings and actions of Rome are inspired by the Holy Spirit. For instance, on the matter of birth control, the Papacy pretty much thought they had put the matter to rest in 1968 with Pope Paul VI's issuance of the encyclical *Humanae Vitae* which ruled against the recommendations of the Poniifical Commission on Birth Control, in forbidding the use of artificial contraception. Unfortunately for the teaching authority of the Magisterium, the laity has almost totally ignored this document, in part because the encyclical itself is flawed by the inability of Church authorities to find a scriptural basis for the Pope's position. Instead the entire document is self-referential. The authority it cites are all pronouncements of other Popes and clergy. It cites no scriptural authority. The Council of Trent, Pope Pius XI's 1930 encyclical *Casti Connubi,* and Pope Pius XII's 1951 Address to Midwives are the primary source documents. Only *Casti Connubi* contains a scriptural reference, and that is the oft repeated misinterpretation of Genesis 38. 8-10, which provides absolutely no firm support to his position.

In *Humani Vitae* there is displayed considerable foresight regarding the possibility of negative social effects flowing from the widespread use of artificial birth control. These are wise and thoughtful observations. However, they are not theological, so when it comes to the heart of the matter, Paul relies solely upon historic precedent, reflecting his fear that if he contradicted his predecessors, he also would be contradicting the Holy Spirit.

This then, is representative of the first of my imponderables: What will be the future of the Catholic church in the face of the paradigm shift in the biological and physical sciences that started with Darwin, Planck, Einstein, LeMaitre, Watson and Crick, and continues at an accelerating pace today? These advances in knowledge, and the correlative changes in the way we perceive and understand the world are even more radical, and even more profound than those of the Enlightenment. Will it be possible for the Christian churches, and specifically, the Catholic church to adjust? Will it be possible for the Catholic church to acknowledge that in the face of new knowledge, the it has unwittingly been the agent of error?

The second big question has to do with the singularity known as the Big Bang. How could it have been possible for all the matter and all the energy of a universe comprising 100 billion galaxies, each made up of 100 billion stars, as well as an even larger mass of dark matter and energy, to have been originally compressed into a single infinitesimal "primeval atom"? It is thought that the explanation is that everything was in the form of pure energy. But, that still begs the question, how can this be?

The third mystery has to do with biological evolution and the question of time. Since it is estimated that cellular life has existed on earth for 3.5 billion years, and multi-cellular life for about 2.5 billion years, how can it be possible that process of random mutations, slowly changing organisms to adapt better to their environment, can produce the incredible complexity encapsulated by the human being, in so short a time? This is especially curious because with increasing size and complexity, the span of generational turnover increases from about 24 hours for the eukaryote, to seven days for the *drosophilia,* to upwards of twenty years for the human, and thus, one must question whether the evolutionary process has had enough time to work its magic.

VIII

Summary of the Argument

- o God exists as creator of the universe
- o God is incomprehensible because of the ontological incongruity between the Creator and the created. Neither His nature nor his attributes can be known.
- o What little we know of God comes solely from Scripture. However, it is possible to glean tiny hints and infinitely small bits of information about God from the creative intuition of poets, prophets, and mystics.
- o An evolutionary principal affecting all physical and biological matter is embedded in creation, enabling its essential teleological direction.
- o Life in the form of prokaryotes, fired by the laws of biological evolution, appeared 3.5–4.2 billion years ago, with Darwinian dynamics producing, as beings become sentient (about one billion years later), the suffering historically associated with the myth of the fall and original sin.
- o God's evolutionary principal is the means by which creation returns to the Creator.
- o There is evil in the universe and it exists in two forms: Natural and Moral.

- Natural evil is the unintended byproduct of the broad evolutionary process in both physical and biological events. Plagues, storms and death are examples of natural evil.
- Moral evil is the freely chosen act of humans doing harm to other humans, to themselves, or to nature itself.
- Moral evil has two levels of intensity:
    - Ordinary Moral evil (sin) which is caused by a person allowing his or her genetically imposed propensity for selfishness to prevail in freely chosen action.
    - Satanic evil, in which the person or the group, allows Satan, often through a perversion of an otherwise morally neutral ideology, to control his or their actions producing extreme harm to others. Most Satanic evil is Big Evil, with an ultimate goal to disrupt and abort creation's teleological return path to God.
- The most pervasive Big Evil of our times is the world-wide mass extinction of humans caused by abortion. However, it is now scientifically demonstrable that human life (as understood by science) begins at conception, and that abortion, at any time in the gestational process, is the taking of human life-a fact to which we should not be indifferent.
- The Incarnation, the Crucifixion, and the Resurrection are God's response to Moral evil in all its varied eruptions.

Bibliography

Alighieri, Dante. *The Divine Comedy.* Translated by Allen Mandelbaum. New York: Alfred A. Knopf, 1995.

Allen, Terrence and Cowling, Graham. *The Cell.* Oxford: Oxford University Press, 2011.

Archibald, John. *Genomics.* Oxford: Oxford University Press, 2018.

Aquinas, Thomas. "Summa Theologica." *Summa of the Summa,* Edited by Peter Kreeft. San Francisco: Ignatius Press. 1990.

Aquinas, Thomas. "Summa Theologica" *Basic Writings of Saint Thomas Aquinas,* Edited by Anton C. Pegis, NewYork: Random House. 1945.

Barr, Stephan M. *Modern Physics and Ancient Faith.* Notre Dame: University of Notre Dame Press, 2013

Bianconi, Eva, Piovesan, Allison et.al. "An Estimation of the Number of Cells in the Human Body'" in *Annals of Human Biology, Volume 40, 2013-issue 6.* Accessed 8/5/2019, https://doi.org/10.3109/0301 4460.2013.807878.

Camus, Albert. *The Plague.* Translated by Colin Duckworth. London: Penguin Books, 2006.

Carroll, Sean B. *The Making of the Fittest.* New York: W.W. Norton & Company, 2006.

Christian, David. *Origin Story: The Big History of Everything.* New York: Little, Brown and Company, 2018.

Collins, Francis S. *The Language of God, A Scientist Presents Evidence For Belief.* New York: Simon $ Schuster, Inc., 2006.

Conn, Walter. *Christian Conversion, A Developmental Interpretation of Autonomy and Surrender.* New York: Paulist Press, 1986.

Crossan, John Dominic. *The Power of Parable.* New York: HarperCollins Publishers, 2012.

Daley, Brian SJ. *Gregory of Nazianzus.* New York: Routledge, 2006.

Darwin, Charles. *Voyage of the Beagle.* London: Penguin Books, 1989. -*The Origin of Species.* London: J.M.Dent & Sons LTD, 1956.

Davis, Brian, OP. *The Reality of God and the Problem of Evil.* London: Continuum International, 2006.

Delio, Illia OSF. "Introduction" in *From Theilhard to Omega, Co-Creating an Unfinished Universe.* Ed. Illia Delio, OSF. Maryknoll, NewYork: Orbis Books, 2014.

Devlin, Thomas M., Ed. *Textbook of Biochemistry: With Clinical Correlations.* New York: John Wiley & Sons, Inc. 2011.

Domning, Daryl P. "Evolution, Evil, and Original Sin". *America Magazine.* November 12, 2001.

Domning, Dayrl P. and Helwig, Monica K. *Original Selfishness: Original Sin and Evil in the Light of Evolution.* NewYork: Routledge, 2016.

Domning, Daryl P. "Theilhard and Natural Selection: A Missed Opportunity" In *Rediscovering Theilhard's Fire*, Edited by Kathryn Duffy SSJ. Philadelphia: Saint Joseph's University Press, 2010.

Fukuyama, Francis. *Our Posthuman Future, Consequences of the Biotechnology Revolution.* New York: Farrar, Straus and Giroux, 2002.

Garrigou-Lagrange, Reginald, O.P. *The One God,* Translated by Dom. Bede Rose O.S.B. St. Louis: B.Herder Book Co. 1943.

Gilbert, Scott F. "Evolution Through Developmental Change," in *Darwin in the Twenty-First Century, Nature, Humanity, and God.* Edited by Philip Sloan, Gerald McKenny, Kathleen Eggleson. Notre Dame: University of Notre Dame Press, 2015.

Gingerich, Owen. *God's Planet.* Cambridge: Harvard University Press, 2014

Haught, John F. *Is Nature Enough? Meaning and Truth in the Age of Science.* Cambridge: Cambridge University Press, 2006.

--*Making Sense of Evolution, Darwin, God, and the Drama of Life.* Louisville, KY: Westminster John Knox Press, 2010.

-- "Theilhard and the Question of Life's Suffering" in *Rediscovering Theilhard's Fire,* Edited by Kathleen Duffy SSJ. Philadelphia: St Joseph's University Press, 2010.

-- *Resting on the Future, Catholic Theology for an Unfinished Universe.* New York: Bloomsbury Publishing Inc., 2015.

Harrington, Joel F. *Dangerous Mystic, Meister Ekhart's Path to the God Within.* New York: Penguin Press, 2018.

Hazen, Robert M. *The Story of Earth: The First 4.5 Billion Years, From Stardust to Living Planet.* New York: Viking Penguin, 2012.

Horn, Stephan Otto and Wiedenhofer. Siegfried. *Creation and Evolution, A conference with Pope Benedict XVI in Castel Gondolfo.* Translated by Michael J. Miller. San Francisco: Ignatius Prsss, 2008.

Hume, David. "Dialogues Concerning Natural Religion" in *The English Philosophers from Bacon to Mill,* Ed. Edwin A. Burtt. New York: Random House, Inc., 1939.

John of Damascus. *Saint John of Damascus: The Fount of Knowledge.* Translated by Frederick H. Chase. Ex Fontibis.com, 2015.

Kolakowski, Leszek. *My Correct Views on Everything,* Edited by Zbigniew Janowski. South Bend: St Augustine's Press, 2005.

Kuhn, Thomas. *The Copernican Revolution* Cambridge: Harvard University Press, 1957.

Milton, John. *Paradise Lost,* Edited by William Kerrigan, and Stephan M. Fallon. New York: Random House, Inc., 2007.

Montini, Giovanni Battista, (Pope Paul VI). *Catechism of the Catholic Church.* Washington: United States Catholic Conference, 1994.

Newman, John Henry. *Apologia Pro Vita Sua.* London: Penguin Books, 2004.

Noble, Dennis. *Dance to the Tune of Life, Biological Relativity.* Cambridge: Cambridge University Press, 2017.

O'Callaghan, John. "Evolution and the Catholic Faith." in *Darwin in the Twenty-First Century, Nature, Humanity, and God.* Edited by by Philip Sloan, Gerald McKenny, Kathleen Eggleson. Notre Dame: University of Notre Dame Press,

Origen. "Commentary on the Epistles to the Romans, Books 1-5", in *The Fathers of The Church*. Translated by Thomas P. Scheck. Washington: The Catholic University Press, 2001.

Pacelli, Eugenio Maria Giuseppe Giovanni, (Pope Pius XII). *Humani Generis,* 1950.

Penrose, Roger. Fashion, Faith, and Fantasy in the New Physics of the Universe. Princeton: Princeton University Press, 2016.

Ratzinger, Joseph C. (Pope Benedict XVI). In the Beginning, A Catholic Understanding of Creation and the Fall, Translated by Boniface Ramsey OP. Grand Rapids, MI: William Erdmans Publishing Company, 1995.

-*Introduction to Christianity,* Translated by J. R. Foster. San Francisco: Ignatius Press, 2004.

Rees, Martin. *Just Six Numbers, The Deep Forces that Shape our Universe,* New York: Basic Books, 2000.

Singh, Sasheela et al. *Abortion Worldwide: A Decade of Uneven Progress.* New York: Guttmacher Institute, 2009.

Slack, Jonathon. *Genes.* Oxford: Oxford University Press, 2014.

Spier, Fred. *Big History and the Future of Humanity,* Second Edition. Chichester UK: John Wiley and Sons, 2015.

Theilhard de Chardin, Pierre. *The Phenomenon of Man.* Translated by Bernard Wall. NewYork: Harper and Brothers Publishers, 1959.

Von Speyr, Adrienne. *Confession,* second edition, Translated by Douglas W. Stott. San Francisco: Ignatius Press, 2017.

Voltaire. *Candide.* Translated and Edited by Robert M. Adams. New York: W.W. Norton and Company, 1991.

Zycinski, Joseph. "Evolutionary Theism and the Emergent Universe" in *Darwin in the Twenty-First Century, Nature, Humanity, and God*, Edited by Philip Sloan, Gerald McKenny, Kathleen Eggleson. Notre Dame: University of Notre Dame Press, 2015.